D1460587

Praise for
Your Stand Is Your Brand

"If you've ever wondered how the practical application of philosophy and values can translate into great success, you will discover it in *Your Stand Is Your Brand*. Patrick Gentempo shares wisdom earned from decades of experience that uniquely aids entrepreneurs and business leaders to create thriving businesses that have a positive impact on the world. I highly recommend it!"

— **John Mackey**, co-founder and CEO of Whole Foods Markets

"Business leaders sometimes see social activism as inconsistent with financial ambition. Patrick Gentempo argues persuasively that social idealism is steroids for entrepreneurial accomplishment, and that a vision rooted in high aspirational values for a compassionate and just society is the most potent platform for consumer appeal and business success."

— **Robert F. Kennedy, Jr.**, activist, environmental attorney, and author of *American Values*

"You are your message, the way you live, the words you say, the actions you take, and the people you surround yourself with. Patrick understands this better than anyone. *Your Stand Is Your Brand* is about bringing that message into the world. I strongly recommend this book."

— **James Altucher**, entrepreneur, venture capitalist, and *Wall Street Journal* best-selling author of *The Power of No*

"For a guy who has spent over 25 years in marketing, hearing all the crap that people are talking about relative to brands, I am excited to share that *Your Stand Is Your Brand* is a message, a process, and a methodology that I personally stand behind. If you care about anything in your life, your business, or your planet, read this book now."

— **Joe Polish**, founder of Genius Network

"Complete success requires more than just biohacking and being a physical badass. It requires a deep look into the mirror and discovering, as Patrick Gentempo puts it, your Miles Davis. *Your Stand Is Your Brand* will take you on a powerful journey into realms where most entrepreneurs don't go, but need to. Completing it is like completing an Ironman triathlon for your mind-set and success."

— **Ben Greenfield**, entrepreneur, biohacker, and *New York Times* best-selling author of *The Low-Carb Athlete*

"It's not often that books can truly cause business breakthroughs. Most are variations of a theme with limited insight. In *Your Stand Is Your Brand*, Patrick Gentempo opens up a parallel universe of possibility for entrepreneurs and business executives that will create quantum leaps in success and effectiveness. Get it, read it, and apply it right now. It may be the best thing you do this year."

— **Garrett Gunderson**, *New York Times* best-selling author of *Killing Sacred Cows* and founder of The Wealth Factory

"The final paragraph on page 31 is worth 100 times what you'll pay for Patrick's book. You may have read 'game-changing' books before, but this one belongs off your bookshelf and on your desk."

— **Alex Mandossian**, entrepreneur and founder of Marketing Online

"Over the many years that I've known Patrick Gentempo, we shared many conversations on business, philosophy, and economics. I've always found his experience, insights, and wisdom to be of great value. In *Your Stand Is Your Brand*, Patrick has translated all this into a book of unique scope and power. Every entrepreneur needs to own it."

— **Paul Zane Pilzer**, economist, social entrepreneur, and *New York Times* best-selling author of *The Next Millionaires*

"There is more to business than profit and loss. With *Your Stand Is Your Brand*, Patrick Gentempo has sparked a new and better era on how business success on all scales can and should be achieved. It's a must-read."

— **Pedram Shojai**, entrepreneur, author of *The Urban Monk*, and founder of Well.Org

YOUR
STAND
IS YOUR
BRAND

Hay House Titles of Related Interest

THE SHIFT, the movie,
starring Dr. Wayne W. Dyer
(available as a 1-DVD program, an expanded 2-DVD set,
and on online streaming video)
Learn more at www.hayhouse.com/the-shift-movie

***

*BRING YOUR WHOLE SELF TO WORK:
How Vulnerability Unlocks Creativity, Connection,
and Performance,* by Mike Robbins

CHILLPRENEUR: The New Rules for Creating Success, Freedom, and Abundance on Your Terms,
by Denise Duffield-Thomas

*HIGH PERFORMANCE HABITS: How Extraordinary
People Become That Way,* by Brendon Burchard

*MILLIONAIRE SUCCESS HABITS: The Gateway to
Wealth & Prosperity,* by Dean Graziosi

*OVERDELIVER: Build a Business for a Lifetime Playing the
Long Game in Direct Response Marketing,* by Brian Kurtz

All of the above are available at your local bookstore,
or may be ordered by visiting:

Hay House USA: www.hayhouse.com®
Hay House Australia: www.hayhouse.com.au
Hay House UK: www.hayhouse.co.uk
Hay House India: www.hayhouse.co.in

YOUR STAND IS YOUR BRAND

How Deciding "Who to Be" (NOT "What to Do") Will Revolutionize Your Business

PATRICK GENTEMPO

HAY HOUSE, INC.
Carlsbad, California • New York City
London • Sydney • New Delhi

Copyright © 2020 by Patrick Gentempo

Published in the United States by: Hay House, Inc.: www.hayhouse.com®
• *Published in Australia by:* Hay House Australia Pty. Ltd.: www.hayhouse
.com.au • *Published in the United Kingdom by:* Hay House UK, Ltd.: www
.hayhouse.co.uk • *Published in India by:* Hay House Publishers India:
www.hayhouse.co.in

Cover design: Charles McStravick
Interior design and illustrations: Nick C. Welch
Photo on page 112 courtesy of: © Dolfo.

All rights reserved. No part of this book may be reproduced by any mechanical, photographic, or electronic process, or in the form of a phonographic recording; nor may it be stored in a retrieval system, transmitted, or otherwise be copied for public or private use—other than for "fair use" as brief quotations embodied in articles and reviews—without prior written permission of the publisher.

The author of this book does not dispense business advice, only offers information of a general nature to help you in your quest for business success. This book is not designed to be a definitive guide or to take the place of advice from a qualified professional, and there is no guarantee that the methods suggested in this book will be successful, owing to the risk that is involved in business of almost any kind. Thus, neither the publisher nor the author assume liability for any losses that may be sustained by the use of the methods described in this book, and any such liability is hereby expressly disclaimed. In the event you use any of the information in this book for yourself, the author and the publisher assume no responsibility for your actions.

Cataloging-in-Publication Data is on file at the Library of Congress

Hardcover ISBN: 978-1-4019-5786-5
E-book ISBN: 978-1-4019-5787-2
Audiobook ISBN: 978-1-4019-5788-9

10 9 8 7 6 5 4 3 2 1
1st edition, March 2020

Printed and bound by CPI Group (UK) Ltd, Croydon CR0 4YY

For my wife, Laurie, who gave me this title
and stands with me, always.
And to my mother, Antoinette,
who shaped me.

CONTENTS

FOREWORD

The world is changing at a dizzying pace, but if you observe most entrepreneurs and businesses today, people seem to be following preset boilerplate templates on what to do and how to show up in life: become the doctor or the engineer, launch the internet start-up, or get venture funding. A graduate from law school will become a partner in a firm. And while these routes are often safe—as millions of people have gone down these career paths and led good, safe lives—these preset routes often pull us away from why we were really born.

I truly believe that every individual is born because they need to express a version of life that is yet to exist or they need to improve the quality of life for other people on this planet. So many of us, though, fail to do so, because rather than truly creating a life and a business and a purpose that is a masterpiece of its own, we move into a life based on preset templates from generations past.

This creates business after business after business that is plain and stays in the shadows and never truly gets to shine its light. But if you look at the greatest entrepreneurial success stories of the world, they often are not about the product, but about what that entrepreneur stood for at the deepest depths of their soul. For example, it wasn't Apple in and of itself that made it a great company. Apple had lived in mediocrity for years when Amelio was ousted, but

Steve Jobs, who stood for design, art, and creativity at a level unparalleled in engineering, brought life and soul to the company.

Then there's Elon Musk and companies like Tesla. Tesla has a market capitalization that is unparalleled in the auto industry, but what makes Tesla, Tesla? It is the soul of the founder and the stand that Elon takes to move humankind to alternative energies so that we can save our planet.

Look at TOMS Shoes, a simple shoe company that became legendary because of its founder, Blake Mycoskie. Blake took a stand to help the poor by giving away a pair of shoes to people who can't afford one every time a consumer buys a pair of shoes from Toms. After its first 10 years of operation, well over 60 million pairs of shoes have been given away to those who were truly in need.

As you look at the most outstanding businesses and individuals in the world today, you'll notice that they shine because they hold firmly to their *stand*. Yet, this quality is rarely touched upon in business schools. It's not something that is discussed with regard to business strategy or marketing, but when applied to business and life, it creates remarkable results.

Taking a stand can feel risky. For example, when Nike took a stand and supported Colin Kaepernick, it resulted in taunts from Donald Trump and a momentary dip in its shares. But very rapidly, Nike shares soared to new heights. Millions of people became renewed Nike fans because Nike chose to stand for something.

A 2018 survey conducted by Edelman found that 64 percent of consumers chose, switched, avoided, or boycotted a brand based on its stand on societal issues. Further, research done in 2018 by the Shelton

Group revealed that 86 percent of consumers believed that companies should take a stand for social issues, and 64 percent of those who said it's 'extremely important' for a company to take a stand on a social issue also stated that they were "very likely" to purchase a product based on that commitment. Based on this research, the Shelton Group asserted that the "CEO Activist" model is becoming more and more powerful.

That is why this book is so important. Somewhere deep inside you, there is a yearning. There is a calling. You are not here to create another company that produces another widget that anyone else can produce. You are here to infuse within your widget or your product or your company, your unique stand. This stand rests on your beliefs, your ideas, your purpose. Your raison d'être. The beliefs, ideas, and gifts that your soul wants you to bring to this world.

Do not deny your spirit its deep longing to express itself within your product, for the world's greatest products and services and businesses are infused with the stand, the values, and the beliefs of its founder. I first heard about Patrick Gentempo when I interviewed him for my education company, Mindvalley. As Patrick spoke about philosophy, he mentioned the phrase, *"Your stand is your brand."* That phrase stuck in my head. It inspired me to reemphasize my beliefs and my values within Mindvalley.

A year later, I was invited to be a guest on *Impact Theory*, hosted by Tom Bilyeu, the famous YouTube personal growth show. Tom asked me, "Are you an entrepreneur or a philosopher?" I quoted Patrick. I said, "It is not the word 'entrepreneur' that defines me, because my businesses come and go, and if I ever were to sell my business or lose my business, God forbid, would that make me less Vishen, or myself? No, it would not. However, if I lost what I stood for, which is unity, I would no longer be Vishen."

I then quoted Patrick again: "Your stand is your brand." It is not what you do that makes you who you are; it is what you believe in the depth of your soul, that which you are willing to stand up for so that you can help push humanity forward. This is what makes you who you are, and when you learn to take this essence and infuse it within your business, that is when magic happens. That is when you step out of the shadows and you become the light. And that is when you will see a whole new level of fulfillment, progress, and growth—not just in your business but in your life.

Vishen Lakhiani
Co-founder and CEO of Mindvalley

INTRODUCTION

Sometimes it takes getting hit by a metaphorical truck to wake you up—to "un-numb" you, and get you thinking deeper so you recognize what is usually hiding in plain sight. I know this because it took a *literal* truck hitting me to come to that realization. Here's what happened . . .

After I graduated chiropractic school in 1983, I started a test-prep business. I had seen firsthand the number of people who attended board review courses and what they cost. The amount of revenue they generated was a matter of simple math. I partnered with my friend and colleague, Dr. Christopher Kent—to this day the best instructor I've ever seen, and whom I poached from the course I'd taken—and the business turned a profit on our very first event. My success with the board review course inspired me to take the next step and open my own practice.

That's when I received a fateful call from my mother. Her tone concerned me at first. She seemed choked up, almost on the verge of tears. I worried someone close to us had died. It turned out she was laughing. "Honey," she said, "you're not going to believe this."

She had submitted my photo to a popular TV show called *The Morning Show*, then hosted by Regis Philbin. They were running a contest called "The Morning Male." My mother was a big fan of the show. Incredibly, out of countless thousands of submissions, I was selected as one of the 10 finalists to appear live on the show at ABC Studios in New York City in front of a celebrity panel of judges in swimsuit and tuxedo. I won. And everything changed overnight.

I received a flood of calls from New York agents wanting to represent me. I began getting scripts for movies and TV shows. I got caught up in the whirlwind, seduced by the promises of fame and fortune. I knew I could run the test-prep business by traveling on weekends, so I picked up and moved to New York City to take acting lessons and prepare for this bold and exciting new direction in my life.

I regularly rode my bicycle to acting classes. On one such occasion, a delivery truck pulled away from the curb halfway out into my lane. I slammed on my brakes, unaware that earlier that morning, another truck had spilled fuel on that same stretch of street. I went down hard. This was at a time before cyclists wore helmets, and I slammed my head on the asphalt, suffering a severe concussion. I skidded for several yards until I was right underneath the front tires of the truck.

It never saw me—and it started to pull out.

The front tires ran over my left leg, breaking it in multiple places. Fortunately, a number of people witnessed what happened and ran to the truck, pounding on the side, getting the driver to stop. Had he continued to pull out of his space, he would have killed me.

After being treated in the emergency room, I was sent home to recover in my apartment. It took little time for depression to set in. Here I was with all this opportunity and excitement around me—things that felt destined to happen—and in an instant, it was gone.

A person can do a lot of soul-searching in times like those, because, truthfully, what else is there to do? I was dizzy from the head trauma, and my leg was elevated to let my fractures heal. I had nowhere to go and nothing to do but read and think.

During that dark time, a question presented itself and would not go away until I answered it.

What the hell am I doing with my life?

I understood how I got swept up in the whole thing. The lifestyle was enticing—but was it really my purpose? Was it truly what I had set out to do? Was it the vision I had for myself?

I had been given a necessary—albeit painful—wake-up call. I had veered far off course from the path of my life. I was swept up in celebrity and attention. I needed to drill down to the deepest core of what my purpose was, and when I did, this situation had been found wanting. Once I had fully recovered, I moved out of the city, back to my parents' home in New Jersey, and got to work setting up a chiropractic practice as I continued with my lucrative board review business.

My discovery of what it was that I had to do—and why—began with a pivotal moment. Yours will, too.

What to Do and Who to Be

Here's the thing: In my heart I *knew* that living in New York and taking acting classes wasn't what I was meant to be doing with my life. Truth be told, I had little talent for acting. It wasn't a natural ability or strength I possessed. That should have been enough of a deterrent, as your true calling lies somewhere within your strengths—not your weaknesses. However, the lure of fame was powerful, and

I convinced myself it was the identity I wanted to adopt, even though at the center of my being, it felt incongruous. It was sexy, but never what I had envisioned for my life.

In all likelihood you've been focused on *what to do* instead of *who to be*.

I know that you likely have had similar experiences—an epiphany where you realized, beyond a shadow of a doubt, what it was you were meant to do in this world. Who you were meant to be. However, somewhere along the way, you went astray.

Let me ask: You know things that you could be doing and are currently not doing that would make your business or life better, right? It's absurd, but everybody does. So, the deeper question is, why aren't you doing what you know? I mean, you and I are together here, right now, to make something better happen. Are you ready to actually make it happen? I hope you are, because the solution is going to be pivotal. It will change your life.

To understand what has been in your way, you must realize that in all likelihood you've been focused on *what to do* instead of *who to be*.

Live Your Values, Take Your Stand

Commit at this moment to understand what it is that prevents you from making your life, your career, or your business thrive. By making this commitment, you can begin to embrace the critical dynamics that affect both start-up entrepreneurial ventures and multibillion-dollar public companies.

To remedy this, you must identify the values that you will never compromise—the stand you will take in this world. All companies, larger ones in particular, are influenced by trends and consumer behavior. Instead, it is vital that you build and run your company, and your life, based on values that align with your *personal* values.

Of course, you run the risk that some people may be turned off by your purpose and your brand. You will alienate some, but at the same time you will be creating a group of enthusiastic supporters who will stay with you forever. So long as you don't compromise your principles and values, are honest and true to who you are, you will build a loyal following and a thriving, sustainable business.

It takes no small amount of courage. The less bold choose to take a middle-of-the-road approach in an attempt to appeal to the broadest audience. In today's marketplace, which values integrity above all, that's the first step toward business demise and personal misery.

Mind if I offer you the option to take a pledge? (No one else will know and it might change your life.) Read this out loud:

> *I pledge to commit to using my experience in reading* **Your Stand Is Your Brand** *to result in a pivotal experience that changes my life.*

Learning How to Think

When I was laid up from my accident, a friend gave me a copy of *The Fountainhead* by Ayn Rand. Rand's integrated view of existence sparked in me a deep interest in philosophy. I've spent the last three-plus decades of my life studying philosophy, and it has made me what I call a "practical philosopher." It has taught me "how to think" and how to apply my thinking as a tool for success in my life.

And in yours.

In this book, I will show you how a lack of thinking and understanding is at the root of your business problems. You'll learn how to leverage your thinking in new and practical ways.

Unfortunately, our educational system doesn't teach us *how* to think, but rather *what* to think. We're taught to be good employees but not business owners and rainmakers. In an era in which we are inundated with data, a structure of how to think is crucial, because data alone is useless. Organized data is merely information. Organized information is knowledge. And organized knowledge is wisdom.

Philosophy, then—a method of organizing your thinking and knowledge—is the path to wisdom and success.

If you think you don't have a philosophy, you're wrong. Everyone has one. It's inescapable. The question is whether or not you've defined it. Leveraged it. Your philosophy is the most practical thing you can hope to embrace, and when I say "practical," I mean "putting dollars in your pocket" practical.

The problem is—to paraphrase Rand—that contradictions in your basic philosophical premises lead to destruction. The amount of destruction is relative to the level of contradiction. Through philosophy, we will identify these contradictions, remove them, and evolve to higher levels of effectiveness. Without the ability to identify these contradictions, you're doomed to be stuck in the same struggles, over and over again.

Let me be clear about one thing, this is *not* a dummy's guide. You are not a dummy! I am not going to insult you by trying to lure you into this book by professing this is so easy any dummy can do it. You are smart—probably smarter than you think. This book is a command to rise through using your mind for what it is—your greatest asset.

My Promise to You

Learning how to use your defined philosophy to identify and eliminate your contradictions will not only help your brand emerge, it will change your life. To this end, I will introduce you to the greatest barrier to entrepreneurial and business growth, which is a state I refer to as "maximum tension."

Once we learn how to break that tension by aligning driving forces, I will teach you about the 5-*P* Expansion Sequence—a five-step model I developed that fully illustrates how philosophy is the ultimate cause, and prosperity is the ultimate effect. I've started numerous successful companies using this model.

To be transparent, not every company I've started has been successful. Far from it. However, the 5-*P* Expansion Sequence greatly increases the probability of success and scaling. I've taught it to thousands of others who have successfully applied it to their own businesses, and I'm excited to share it with you.

Once you understand the 5-*P* Expansion Sequence, I'm going to teach you how to unleash the true power of philosophy in business. It is the most fundamental thing any entrepreneur needs to understand in order to fulfill their true potential and capacity for what's possible in business.

The next step will be to go almost uncomfortably deep with a startling concept I call "finding your Miles Davis." It will get you to think and self-observe at levels you likely never have before.

Finding your Miles Davis will bring you one step closer to targeting your brand purity—bringing you one step closer to developing your stand. It will allow you to make your brand so pure that it becomes irresistible for the people who share your values.

Once your brand purity is locked in, it's time to seek some spectacular, world-changing breakthroughs. I've identified a simple sequence, called "anatomy of a breakthrough," that you can replicate on purpose, as opposed to hoping for a happy accident someday.

If you don't already think I'm crazy, you will when, after I've shown you how to create all this success, I show you how to burn it all down to become even *more* successful. It's a process I refer to as "creative destruction," and it's all about how the best time to reinvent yourself is when you're at the height of your success. A number of world-famous brands have done this, and perhaps soon, you will, too.

Taking *My* Stand

It's easy to talk about standing for something without putting some skin in the game. How often in life or in business have we gotten advice or direction from people who don't practice the principles they espouse? Far more frequently than we can measure, it seems. This book and the principles contained within it were born from the experience of taking my own personal stands, at great risk to my career—and the results were staggering.

I was once at a medical science and research conference in Washington, DC. A Nobel Laureate took the stage and spoke about the fact that genetically modified foods were a huge breakthrough in science and would end world hunger. He went on to say that the anti-GMO movement was made up of a bunch of crazy, unscientific conspiracy theorists who had no science to back up their concerns and that they needed to be fought against.

I knew better, and wanted to make sure others knew, too.

But who was I to point a finger at a Nobel Laureate and say, "He's wrong. Dead wrong!"? We went to work. We took a stand. It was "business activism."

I partnered with Jeff Hays, an uncommonly talented documentary filmmaker and an exceptional human being. Together, we co-founded a film company, Revealed Films, to set the record straight about various controversial issues affecting health and wellness. We certainly had the hope that this project would be profitable but understood that the probability was likely low.

We knew there were eminent experts and scientists who were willing to speak out. We knew that the public was being lied to—misled—and that people were getting sick and dying as a result. According to one study published in a peer-reviewed journal, over eighteen billion pounds (yes, that's billion with a *B!)* of glyphosate, the extremely toxic chemical sprayed on GMO crops, has gone into the environment. This water-soluble poison was, to us, the biggest environmental catastrophe in history. We also knew we were up against a multibillion-dollar corporation, Monsanto, that was legally fierce—lethal even.

Jeff and I set out with an impossible agenda to get the whole docuseries filmed, edited, and launched in under three months. We worked nonstop. I went from having a mature business experience to being on the ground day and night, seven days a week, like a start-up entrepreneur. All along the way, as we let people know about our endeavor, I was called horrible names because children all over the world were going to starve due to the "misinformation" I was spreading about GMOs, Roundup, and the cancer-causing agent contained in it—the poisonous glyphosate. I was called a conspiracy theorist. I was told that taking on the likes of a huge and powerful corporation, Monsanto, was career suicide.

I would not be deterred. Not this time. I had to take my stand. Of course, I was scared. But I believed too deeply in my values to be discouraged.

It ended up being an adventure and one of the most fun experiences I had ever had in business. It took me to amazing places and introduced me to other "stand-takers"—people who were very smart, very committed, and were willing to tell the truth publicly. Some of them became close, personal friends. This venture and the company as a whole turned out to be the most successful year-one start-up business I'd ever been involved with—number one out of the sixteen or so businesses I've started in my life. In its first twelve months, the company generated $4 million in revenue and brought $1 million to the bottom line.

A little over a year after we released *GMOs Revealed*, we were vindicated. A legal team that included a very courageous stand-taker, Robert F. Kennedy, Jr., got Monsanto in court on behalf of a plaintiff who was dying from non-Hodgkin's lymphoma. They asserted that his illness was caused by its product, Roundup. He was a groundskeeper at a school.

The jury awarded him a staggering $289 million. Most of this was punitive as they asserted that Monsanto knowingly marketed a dangerous product. Plaintiffs in other similar trials had been awarded tens of millions with the jury's finding that Monsanto acted with "malice or oppression." In one case, there was a $2 billion award.

It's hard to describe the internal experience when you take a great deal of heat and are accused of heinous things, and then live to see the truth being exposed in light of day, thereby vindicating you.

At the time of this writing, there are more than eleven thousand additional lawsuits pending against Monsanto. However, there are countless more souls whose lives have been devastated due to corporate greed and perpetrated lies—and that causes me great sadness.

Polarization always has two sides. While I had my fair share of detractors, I gained an equal—if not greater—number of supporters. It was because I took a stand and decided that I would not equivocate.

I don't tell you this because I want you to agree with my stance. This book is not about trying to change your mind on any particular health or environmental issues. You don't have to agree with my position. What is critical is that you understand the importance—and the value—of drawing a line in the sand about that which you believe in. It doesn't have to be in epic, David and Goliath–type battles of life and death. You can take a stand on anything you find important. If you do it with integrity and passion, incredible success will follow. It happened for me.

I wrote this book so it can happen for you.

Going "All In" and Having a Pivotal Experience

What's your highest intention—your best hope—for what might happen as a result of you and I spending all this time together?

It's important to recognize that by reading this book, you're approaching a potential inflection point. This book is intended to lead you to the pivotal moment in your life, the delivery truck that puts you on a new path. It will be transformational—but let me be clear, this only happens if you fully immerse yourself in this process and commit to having a pivotal experience in advance of reading the rest of this book.

How many business and personal development books have you read before this one? How many highlights cover the pages of those books? Do they still sit on your shelves or in boxes, untouched gathering dust? (By the way, I know this because I was *guilty as charged* till I woke up!) Will you ever *truly* implement all those strategies to make your life better? I've spent a lot of years on that *self-help junkie merry-go-round*, so I know it well. I was always convinced that the next book or seminar held the key for me to finally break through to the next level.

When it comes to books and seminars and other such investments of time, money, and energy, most of us get what I like to call the "hot tub experience." When you're stiff and sore, a hot tub feels great when you're in it. You're warm and relaxed, and everything feels right with the world. When you step out and dry off, you might still feel some of the effects. The next morning, though? Your life hasn't changed. The warm water and bubbles had no lasting impact. It just felt good at the time.

If you think this book is going to solve your problems or change your life just by reading it, then you're setting yourself up for another hot tub experience. And even though I enjoy hot tubs pretty frequently (I live in a ski town), my purpose in writing this book was to deliver to you something pivotal. Life changing.

I'm operating under the assumption that you didn't buy this book because you had nothing better to do. This is not a work of fiction designed to whisk you away to some imaginary world and provide you with a distraction from the very real effort you need to make. My strategies are battle-tested and proven to work—but you cannot go halfway. If you can go *all in* on these concepts and strategies—if you can have a *pivotal* experience—then in twenty years you will look back and say, "Since I read that book, I was put on a new and better path I otherwise would have never taken." This book will provide that level of transformation for you—*if* you put in the energy.

Now that you know what you're in for, it's time to break the tension—the *maximum tension*, that is; the curse that holds back entrepreneurs and businesses from their greatest level of success.

It's time to take a stand.

Chapter One

MAXIMUM TENSION

So why *do* entrepreneurs not do the things they already know that would make their lives better? For a part of my childhood, my father was a struggling entrepreneur. Prior to that, he had a very high-level executive job that called for extensive travel, taking him away from our family frequently. I remember clearly, when I was around eight years old, he came home from work and announced that he had quit his job. The idea to leave had been brewing in his mind for a couple of years. He knew that he was not doing what he was meant to do, and he didn't like being away from his family so much.

He always had a passion for natural health—vitamins, supplements, and health foods—which was a somewhat unusual perspective back in the 1970s. There were no GNCs. There was no culture aligned with eating organic foods. So, after leaving his corporate job and thinking about it for a long while, he decided to open up a health-food store in the small town of Ramsey, New Jersey, where I grew up. He was far ahead of his time. Today we call this "the bleeding edge."

Operating as a solopreneur, he worked seven days a week, chasing his passion for many years—and for every one of those years, he struggled. He never actually made any money. In fact, I can remember bill collectors calling our home. Somehow, he managed to make ends meet, but he never got to a point where the store became a truly profitable venture. It never provided any real financial security. What amazes me is that he never transferred that stress to the kids. To me and my older brother and sister, things seemed just fine. In hindsight, I can't imagine the burden he felt.

Finally, after several years, he had to shut the store down. He was fortunate enough to find a job he really liked with the county, working as a training instructor at the police and fire academy.

In the meantime, while I was in high school, I had met fathers of two friends of mine. These men were successful and very wealthy. They lived in large homes, drove expensive cars, flew first class, and took great vacations. They were businessmen—entrepreneurs who owned their own companies, and the companies were scaled up. They produced significant revenue. They were millionaires. When around them, I would constantly ask them questions any chance I got to understand just what it was they were doing to achieve what they had.

It was, in a sense, the "rich dad, poor dad" scenario: My father owned his own business and was struggling, whereas my friends' fathers were wealthy. What had they figured out that he hadn't? Let's be clear. I loved my father (he has since passed). I wouldn't trade him for any other father in the world. We had a great relationship and I learned so many things from him, and although he disagreed with many of my business decisions, he was always there to support me in any way he could.

I also recognized that these successful men had something to teach me—that they understood something he did not. As a young and impressionable teenager, these men took me under their wings and talked to me about their businesses. I would stay up, sometimes for hours, talking to them, and they liked the fact that I took such a vested interest in what they were doing. Interestingly enough, they didn't tutor me on balance sheets and P&Ls. They focused on their philosophy of business, particularly on headspace and what it takes to succeed.

And I ate up every word of it.

In these conversations, I homed in on a common theme that both men independently pointed out—a theme that is still pervasive in books and success seminars. It is a foundational premise that in today's world has become a personal development and success mantra, and I had to learn the hard way that this belief element—which is a catchphrase that had become a meme in the entrepreneurial world—is about as destructive a concept as one can imagine. It gets adopted without critical consideration.

This is why the practical use of philosophy is hypercritical. The problem is people, without thinking much about them, adopt premises from other people who haven't thought enough about them. As much as these early mentors thought they were sharing deep wisdom and wanted to help me, their lack of critical thinking in some of the ideas they fed me hurt me, and taken to the extreme, could have killed me.

Success Requires Sacrifice

"If you want to really be successful," they told me, "if you want to get ahead of everybody else, you're going to have to sacrifice. That means that you're going to be working weekends while your friends are out partying or playing. It means that you're going to have a lot of late nights. You're going to have to put in that extra time, the extra effort, and the extra energy it takes to succeed at another level. It is what other people are simply unwilling to do. The more you are willing to sacrifice, the more success you will create."

When you start to break this down, even though there are some valid aspects, there are a number of contradictions here.

Sacrifice Equals Pain

The fundamental theme that success requires sacrifice was baked into my mind by these highly successful men who had effectively become my early mentors.

The implication was that *more* success required *more* sacrifice. Therefore, sacrifice was a value I embraced as an entrepreneur. As a value creator. As someone who was committed to uncommon success. I wanted to compete and win. Sacrifice had this mythic, romantic quality to it. Thus, I began my own entrepreneurial life believing the bigger my businesses grew, the more sacrifice it required.

In my twenties, I was on a mad tear. My chiropractic practice was growing. While in that practice, I co-developed diagnostic technologies that I later received patents for, and we started up a diagnostic technology company. From there, I realized that it wasn't the technology we were selling that gets the results in the business, but *who* the person is that uses it that gets the results. So, we developed business training programs and other educational and service ventures.

Between my chiropractic practice, the diagnostic technology company, and the other affiliated business divisions we were bringing to life, I was working seven days a week for years and never took a vacation. I was young and single at the time, so not only was it feasible, but I loved every minute of it.

Eventually, I sold my practice. It was a poignant time as it required an identity shift for me, the first of a few such shifts over my lifetime. I went full-time as the CEO of the diagnostic technology company, operating it, and with that traveled over 150 thousand miles per year with the perpetual quest of growing it. We were really succeeding in a visible way, and in my little world, I was becoming very well known.

During the course of building these businesses, I did find time to fit in some semblance of a personal life. I had relationships for varying periods of time that failed, but at one point, I found myself married with three young children. I fancied myself a good husband and father because I was such a good provider. I suddenly realized that while I was building this business and building a family, I was in a great deal of pain. It was a subconscious kind of pain—I wasn't acutely aware of it—but it was there all the same.

My level of fitness was far below what I wanted it to be. I was once a national champion athlete and I was getting out of shape. I was spending less and less time with Laurie, my wife. There were so many late nights and so much travel that I hardly saw her. I wasn't spending much time with my young kids. In the back of my mind, I told myself when they were older and it would matter more, I'd do more with them. My businesses and their growth were my single-minded obsession. Sacrifice was the driving virtue.

Wasn't it plain to see? From business and financial success, all else could follow.

It's amazing how we can rationalize things.

The other values I held in my life—my love relationship, my parenting, my personal health and wellness, my spirituality—were all, in an unspoken sense, distractions to this fast-moving train that was the development and revenue growth of my businesses. If they didn't want to get destroyed, they had to get out of the way and accept a sacrificial role, because that train had left the station and it was committed to reaching its destination.

It's important to note that for me, the rocket fuel that drove these businesses was *purpose*. I was, and still am, totally purpose-driven. I had a vision for my profession and a vision for the world—and it was a significant one. Being purpose-driven is a huge virtue, but it can also be a package deal. Why? Because many times there is a profound sense of righteousness when facing your sacrifices. If I am changing and saving lives on an ever-expanding scale, who or what should be so selfish as to get in the way of that?

It took teaching my clients who were other business owners about the practical applications of philosophy—particularly about contradictions and destruction—for me to finally reach a point where I had to face my own contradictions if I was going to relieve the deepening pain I was experiencing.

The specific lesson I had been teaching—an edict I had learned from reading the writings of Ayn Rand and further developed with my intellectual mentor, Dr. Nathaniel Branden—was that *contradictions in your philosophical premises lead to destruction*—and the amount of destruction is relative to the level of the contradiction. This is especially applicable to entrepreneurs but applies to everyone.

The way to overcome the pain and limitation contradictions cause is to identify those contradictions and
resolve them. The resultant outcome is always increased
expansion, flow, and joy. This is where applied philosophy
comes in as an unmatched tool of practicality. Identifying
values comes from the third branch of philosophy—ethics. (More on these branches and how to apply them in
the next chapter.) Becoming conscious of your personal
values and business values and creating alignment is a
nonnegotiable essential.

**The way to overcome the pain and limitation contra-
dictions cause is to identify those contradictions and
resolve them.**

I was teaching this lesson at a popular immersion-
style boot-camp training program hosted by my
company. We would hold six to eight of these a year
for our clients. I was far away from home, deep in the
Colorado Rockies on a 6,000-acre ranch at an 8,600-
foot altitude. Cell phones don't work there. There
were no phones or TVs in the cabins we slept in. My
premise was that you can't get real transformation in
hotel convention centers. You needed to be removed
from all that, break all patterns, and immerse. In that
environment, with days starting at 7:00 A.M. and going
sometimes past midnight, it stretches you and creates
space for something magical to happen.

After a lecture, I returned to my room. While I sat
there alone, I realized how much pain I was experiencing
in my own life beyond just my business. In fact, my business was quite successful—so much so that I was contemplating growing it to the next level again and expanding

it. This expansion included the acquisition of a company with two offices on the West Coast, in Seattle and San Diego. My offices were on the East Coast, in the suburbs of Manhattan. I had actually gotten quite far down the road in negotiations of this deal.

The acquisition had very favorable terms and, strategically, it made a lot of sense. Organic growth of my company was slowing as it inevitably does. So, a strategic acquisition of a product company that we could likely quadruple in size just by marketing to our existing client base was a no-brainer.

However, it would have added even more travel to an already hectic schedule. It would have required a significant increase in intensity necessary to integrate one company into another—training the employees, reorganizing operations and removing redundant positions (this meant layoffs, which are never fun), merging finance, sales, and marketing, just for starters. It would add up to an enormous amount of additional time, as I would have to lead all those efforts. Of even greater consequence, it would further drain my energy, so even when I was home, I would be hollow and spent.

As I envisioned the growth of the companies, I stepped outside of myself to look more objectively at what I was doing. There I was sitting alone in a room, far away from my family, teaching other business owners who were chiropractors with a purpose. I thought of my kids and my wife spending so many nights alone. Even when I was home, I was still at the office late. I'd return to the house only to have to do some additional work before I went to bed. I was exhausted much of the time. With all this, the concept of expanding the business made me sick to my stomach.

It's important to point out that had I been in the office in my normal routines, I don't know that I would have had this moment of clarity. There's an old saying that when you are up to your ass in alligators, it's hard to remember that your mission is to drain the swamp. I had to get out of the swamp to see things clearly and to *feel* my life. In the alligator pit, you can get pretty numb.

I had to ask myself, *Where did I go wrong? Why am I experiencing this pain? Where is my contradiction?*

Identify *Your* Contradiction

It became necessary for me to do what I was teaching others to do: identify my contradiction. Why did I feel stretched, almost to a breaking point, where I felt like my body might quite literally split in half? I had a major blind spot that I felt could tear my life apart—I might get sick, end up divorced, or become a stranger to my children.

By all appearances, I was a rising star, becoming extremely popular and well known in my profession. I was growing a successful business that was having a massive impact on the world, and I was motivating the masses. From the outside, I looked like I had it all. I loved what I was doing, but I didn't love how I was living, and that raised important questions for me—as they should for you.

What view of reality, what premise was I holding that was in contradiction to my values and leading me on the destructive path I was on? What were my premises around business success? What was it that drove my thinking and actions when it came to creating higher levels of success in my business? What was driving me?

I thought about the conversations I'd had back during high school with my friends' fathers, my original mentors, those men whom I viewed as successful. I admired them—I still do for many reasons. What did they instill in me? That success required sacrifice. As I reviewed my behavior in hindsight, it was exactly the message I was embodying, even though I wasn't consciously aware I was doing it. I was sacrificing like crazy.

The Power of the Premise

Premises are quite powerful. The right ones will take you to the life of your dreams, the wrong ones will destroy your life, and "mixed" premises will keep you on a rollercoaster ride that you'll desperately want to get off of, but alas, you can't seem to.

When I identified that I held the premise that success requires sacrifice, every single time I wanted to grow my business to the next level—which was essentially every quarter of every year—I was subconsciously looking around and asking, *What do I need to sacrifice to make that happen?*

Sacrifice is a very misunderstood concept. Many erroneously see it as a virtue. Sacrifice, by its very definition, means trading something of greater value for something of lesser value. If I give you a dollar and you give me back a quarter, I just sacrificed seventy-five cents. The new acquisition of those West Coast businesses would have meant significant personal sacrifices—even less time with my wife and children and even less time for me to take care of myself, to be healthy and fit.

Notice these are all values and how my actions were in contradiction to these values. More on this later.

Though it took me longer than it probably should have, I now realized that the parts of my life that were in pain were the victims of a sacrifice that I perceived as necessary for me to grow my business. Up to now, this was unconscious and playing in the background, but now I could see it clearly. With that epiphany, I decided to delete the flawed and destructive premise, that success requires sacrifice. I was done sacrificing. Instead, I consciously chose a new one to replace it with.

The new premise?
I told myself: *I could have it all!*

This meant that I could have a legendary love affair with my wife, I could be an extraordinary father to my children, and I could have a growing, thriving, and successful business. I could be remarkably healthy and fit, look and feel great as I advanced every year, and have a centered and fulfilling spiritual life. These were all the things that I wanted.

I adopted this premise knowing full well it wasn't going to be easy. I didn't get to say "I'm going to have it all" and then have it instantly be so. However, I knew that I had no chance of it ever coming to fruition if I didn't first start with the premise that it was *possible*. If that wasn't a part of my fundamental philosophy, then I would never have it all. I made the choice to believe it could happen. In doing so, instead of looking for things to sacrifice every day of my life in order to achieve success, I looked for strategies that allowed me to have it all *without* making sacrifices. Let that sink in for a moment.

Much to everyone's surprise, I backed out of the acquisition deal. I told myself that I would find a different way to grow my business that did not involve me sacrificing everything that was important to me.

The company that was up for sale was in trouble. I knew we could help it by acquiring it and that it held a lot of opportunity for us. There were two owners and I worked for almost a year on the game plan for what I would do with the company and how I could grow it. I shared with the two owners everything I would have done to not only save their business, but to greatly expand it.

Over the next few years, that company became quite large, producing between $35 million and $50 million in annual revenue, to some extent because of the support I lent them during their growth period. However, not once did I look back on that as a bad decision. I was happy for their success, and I was especially glad that I had not made the move to acquire them, as it would have potentially cost me my marriage, my health, and my relationship with my children. I found a win-win through a strategic relationship instead of an acquisition. I was working to find ways to have it all. The new premise equaled new creative thinking—a healthier framework, new solutions to problems, and a new personal paradigm that excited me.

The power of the practical application of philosophy was changing everything.

A State of Maximum Tension

In the opening pages of this book, I introduced you to the idea that we already know things that we could be doing to improve our lives or our success in business. Yet we aren't *doing* those things. We go out and continuously seek new information, new ideas, and new strategies with the intention to grow and expand on our success—and yet we don't act to use the information we already have. It's an absurdity with deep implications.

When I lectured to audiences on these subjects, I thought deeply about what it was people needed to hear in order to move them to action and apply what they just learned. It was clear that it was an issue related to motivation—but not in the way you might think.

It's really more about *motive forces.*

What is the nature of human motivation? Why do some people who have a sincere desire to improve their lives—and know how to do it—fail to follow through? Even as those same people try to discover new methods to improve their lives, they still don't act.

As I continued to contemplate why this occurred, and gained deeper awareness from my work with clients and public speaking, the answer to the question became clear: People don't do the things they know would improve their lives because they are existing in a state of what I call "maximum tension." When you truly understand what I mean by maximum tension and learn to remedy it, you will open up space in your life that possesses the inherent potential to take you to the next level. Getting this figured out all boils down to a simple three-word question: *What drives you?*

Even though this is a simple question, it is not an *easy* question. There are so many unnamed driving forces at active and persistent play in our life that there's no immediate way to identify, assess, and modify them all at once. It's a process of living consciously and that requires long-term discipline. However, when we are in crisis and things are falling apart, there's an opportunity to find some key contradictions in your driving forces.

For example, imagine right now that whatever is driving you in your personal life is pulling you in an easterly direction. Now imagine that whatever is driving you in your career is pulling you to the west. To get a "mind's eye" visual on this, let's say that when you are getting pulled "east," your left arm starts raising from your side, while the westerly forces start raising your right arm. As these forces keep driving in opposite directions, you can for a period of time support the opposing forces as you keep raising each arm to a point where they are completely extended outward. At that point, you are on a cross—you can't go further in either direction.

You're stuck. You're in pain. You're at *maximum tension.*

There is no space to do anything new. As you try to move east, the tension of the forces pulling you west won't let you move, and vice versa.

To take this metaphor further and illustrate the complexity of human motivation and action, now imagine that you have arms 360 degrees around your body. These arms are now also pulling and pointing in opposing directions toward your parenting, your spirituality, your finances, and your love relationship—all of the dimensions of your life, all at once. Once you reach the point of maximum tension, there is *no space* for you to add anything new. If at this stage I were to give you a fantastic new business tactic to put into action, you couldn't. You are already too overwhelmed by all the other forces and dimensions pulling at you. There's simply no room for new ideas and actions, no matter how revolutionary it might be for you.

Worse yet, if you try to force new things—new energy, if you will—into a system that is at maximum tension, the system will break apart. We've all seen people get sick, get divorced, have seriously painful things happen in their life because they took a system at maximum tension—aka their life—with significant contradictions fully manifested, and then tried to drive it further without first correcting it.

Once you understand maximum tension and can identify it in yourself, what are your choices? The first choice is to stay stuck, stressed, and in pain. You'll have transient ups and downs. You'll go to more seminars and read more books hoping for a breakthrough, but year in and year out, nothing really changes. Life is about trying to keep all the balls in the air.

Often, people who have maximum tension as a blind spot try to force growth into one area when crisis occurs. They'll say to themselves, *Oh my God, I have to save my marriage,* and they force new activities and strategies into their marriage *while still in maximum tension*—and they do so at the expense of their business. It begins to fall apart as a result. There is no new alignment—just a reshuffling of the deck chairs on the *Titanic.*

Sadly, I've seen this happen many times. Marriages break apart, and business owners wind up estranged from their children. I've seen relatively young people have heart attacks, and even die, trying to force a system to move while at maximum tension. I've personally experienced varying versions of this, but fortunately my study in applied philosophy saved me.

Entrepreneurs are good at force, and force is the impulse when things start to get bad. We want to assert a force of will to make things the way we want them. Force in this situation, however, is not good. Force will break things. A few years back, I remember writing in my journal once while at maximum tension, in pain, and experiencing the impulse to unleash the force of my will. I was overcommitted with multiple businesses that were all requiring my attention. A managing partner didn't work out. A key employee left for another business. Some debt was creating additional pressure. I was gearing up for full "fight mode" with anger driving me to want to kick some ass.

Fortunately, I took a moment to center myself so I could write. I put a little space mentally between my challenges and myself, and in observing myself in the situation, I wrote, *If you want a fight to the death, you'll get it.*

I was a bit startled by what I wrote. I backed off and got smarter. Once I got out of the fight-or-flight mode, I could start to observe contradictions, and without force, I could rearrange them like chess pieces on a board so that they aligned.

I don't mean to make this sound easy. It's not—but it's important to understand, in the energetic world, the world of thought and observation and contemplation, the place where you form your philosophy that precedes your physical actions, that force is an ugly thing. The proper alternative is creating alignment for ease and flow. It's about releasing tension, not adding it.

Release the Tension

So, what's the solution?

You must identify the driving forces in the key areas of your life. Rather than having them oppose each other, thereby reaching that maximum tension point, you have to step back and reorganize to align those forces. When you do that, and then put energy into that system, you get explosive positive movement. Going back to the image we created together earlier, imagine your outstretched arms that are east and west, suddenly coming into alignment in front of you, both pointing north. Now you put energy into that system and growth is explosive!

Have you ever noticed that growth—whether in your relationships, in your health and fitness, or in your business—is rarely *only* incremental all of the time? You *can* get incremental growth, but it is hardly ever constant. What typically happens is you have a breakthrough—some new realization that comes into your experience—and you go from point A to point B at the speed of light instead of crawling one step at a time. Why? Because what typically happens is that you have identified something that takes things that were in conflict and aligns them, or you eliminated something unnecessary that was out of alignment with something critical. When you put your energy into aligning those things instead of breaking them apart, it lurches forward. You have a sudden advancement that takes you to the next level.

For example, I once was consulting with a large, multimillion-dollar chiropractic business. Although they were doing well, they had been stuck at the same level for too long and were starting to burn out. During the "war room" process, we unpacked a lot of "stuff" and could observe emerging contradictions.

The core values of the business were totally confused. The purpose was stated, but it wasn't compelling. The two partners in the business were not synced up on any of these things. As we started to dig through these items and got the partners to reveal what their fundamental view of reality was relative to the services they were providing, what values they were aligned with, and what the clear purpose of the business was, something strong and focused started to happen. They started seeing that they were trying to diversify the revenue lines of the practice, seeing these things as an opportunity, but in reality, many of these things were not aligned with what they stood for. For example, they had an entire part of the business dedicated to massage services. Even though massage is a good thing, it was not core to their purpose. All the management of the employees, scheduling, and other energy that went into it were drawing it away from where the real passion was.

Also, they were renting out parts of their office and staff to support other providers to add revenue. But when they really thought about it, they didn't share the philosophy or values of these other providers they were putting right into their space!

There were diagnostics and treatments they were doing that were "just an opportunity," but were contradictory to what their purpose was. So, what do you do? These revenue lines were a pretty good chunk of their total revenue. They were also the things keeping them stuck, stressed, and burning out.

They shut down massage entirely. They parted ways with the providers that weren't core to their purpose and aligned with their values. They ceased all services and selling any products out of the business that weren't *completely* aligned. To further the metaphor from earlier, they took all the arms pointing in contradictory directions, unshackled them, and got everything pointing in one unified direction.

This, of course, is very disruptive. But disruption was completely necessary. By making these corrections, they "squatted" a bit, seeing revenue shrink while making the corrections. But once they dialed it in, they had breakthrough growth to new levels. They had more margin on the revenue. And perhaps most importantly, they ignited a passion in themselves as the business owners that was nowhere to be found before.

Sounds great, right? So how does it work?

First, you must identify the important categories within your life. As an easy starting point, I like to begin with just four of them. For reference, my wife, Laurie, and I have dear friends Jon and Missy Butcher who are the founders of Lifebook, a very powerful personal development system that identifies twelve categories. So, for the sake of simplicity, we'll discuss four, but know that you can take it much further.

1. Personal Life

I define your personal life as you, separate from the rest of the world. It represents your needs and your values independent of your interaction with other people. For example, your health and fitness—when you're exercising, you do it alone. Your personal development activities would go here as well. My study of the practical application of philosophy, for example, would go here. Your hobbies and other passions would also be included. What premises do you have around all these things and how are they driving you in your life? Are they aligned or competing with other things?

2. Relationships

Your relationship life can be broken down into multiple subcategories—your love relationship, parenting, friendships, and others. However, for the sake of this exercise, let's consider the concept of relationships as a whole. While it might be tempting to distill it down to specifics, let's assume you have certain values around relationships, and that's what you'll want to identify. I will say, for me, the most significant breakthroughs when removing contradictions came in my love relationship. When that gets aligned with career and everything else, be ready for happiness and fulfillment that you probably don't have a premise or a context for.

3. Career and Finances

Career and finances are closely related. Your personal wealth and career have an obvious connection, but they are, in fact, separate things. For example, there were many times in my personal experience where what I wanted to do with my businesses and career threatened my personal wealth. It's called risk-taking. It's called being an entrepreneur. I have certainly placed some bets that translated into painful losses. My dear friend and longtime accountability partner Rick Sapio calls that "tuition." Looking through that lens helps to take some of the sting out of it. Sometimes people inherit wealth that is unrelated to their career, but for simplicity's sake, let's keep career and finance together for now.

4. Spirituality

What type of a spiritual experience do you want to have in your life and what are your values around that? Are their certain practices or rituals that bring fulfillment? Prayer? Meditation? Getting quiet and connecting? It's different for each individual, but in my mind, important to everyone. Personally, I can tell you with time and contemplation, this area continues to evolve for me and increases in importance.

A recent trip to Israel on a film project had a major impact. I've developed new premises around the role of faith in human life. My younger, more arrogant self saw faith as a sign of weakness. I certainly respected others' choice to be faith-based, but for me, my intellectual life, to a large extent, dismissed it. With time, however, as Hemingway once said, "Eventually life breaks everyone."

We are mortal. We perceive our morality, yet we don't have objective knowledge about how we got here and where, if anywhere, we are going. In essence, we are all orphans who don't know who our parents are. Neurobiologically speaking, we are wired for faith. So, now I have new premises around faith, and I work to align them with my career, marriage, parenting, and all the rest.

Creating Alignment

Now that we've identified a starter list of four important categories in your life, let's work with them in an exercise to release tension and get them aligned.

The key things to identify in each area of your life are premises—or belief elements—and values. These come from two different branches of philosophy that we'll discuss in the next chapter. A premise is a view of reality that you operate from. In part, it defines the boundaries of what's possible. A value is something that you strive to achieve and keep.

Let's revisit the physical image of you standing with your arms stretched out toward east and west. Your identified values and their required actions for attainment are in contradiction with each other. As you resolve this and begin to create alignment between the values in your four categories, your arms come in front of you, in parallel, pointing north. With that alignment, you put new energy into that system, and your progress takes off like a shot. Doing this resolves the tension, allowing you to grow rather than be stuck in one place.

I understand this sounds a bit abstract, so let me provide you with two examples to help make this more concrete.

Let's say that my top *value* in my personal financial category is financial freedom, while my top *value* in my career category is self-funded growth and expansion—meaning that I don't want to have partners in my business or give up equity. I want to wholly own the business because my value is that working with partners or minority shareholders is too troublesome. The implication is that I have to constantly take all the risk and make all of the investments in the company, and with that I have the upside of not having to share any of it or deal with anyone else. It is important to note that this example thus far presupposes that I know what my top values are. Figuring that out is more than half the battle.

You can instantly see a conflict between these two values: financial freedom on one hand and taking all the risk on the other. It's not that one is right and the other is wrong, but when you put them together, they create tension. If I get to a point where my value of financial freedom—which means an accumulated amount of liquidity that keeps me free—wins out, I'm going to stop funding the growth of my company. If the value of my self-funded growth and expansion of the business wins out, I'm going to be taking my liquidity and risking it in the business. One of these two values is going to end up in trouble, which creates tension and conflict within me.

I have to ask myself: How can I take these two conflicting values and develop new values that would make them align?

One way would be to let go of the value of self-funded growth and expansion and open myself to the idea of using other people's money. Perhaps I can sell 30 percent of the company, take a large portion of that transaction, and put it in my pocket so I have financial freedom, then put the rest of the money into the company for its growth and expansion. Yes, it means the involvement of a minority shareholder, but I would achieve company growth and financial freedom with an adjustment of my values.

As another example, let's say that one of my top values is to achieve financial freedom by age fifty. That says, "Okay, I value financial freedom but do not have to have it today." I'm going to keep pushing my chips into the center of the table while I'm in my thirties and forties to keep growing this company. Then, when I turn fifty, I'll want to make sure that I'm pivoting my value to having financial freedom and security now so that business growth and expansion become a lesser value at *that* point in my career.

Now, let me share with you an example of aligning *values* and *premises* in my personal life.

Previously, I mentioned the pain I was in earlier in my career. I was married, with three young children, and growing demanding entrepreneurial businesses that I loved. My wife, Laurie, and I would discuss our relationship values and the critical priority of staying connected through all the chaos. So, to align actions with those values, we had a weekly date night, rhythmic trips without the kids, and other such things. We also had a premise around how we needed to operate to succeed and reach our goals. The premise, the view of reality, was that our goals require us to, wait for it, "divide and conquer." Ever hear that before? If the *value* is to stay connected, can you do that operating with a "divide and conquer" view of reality?

Needless to say that even with our actions, date night and so on, we still were falling short of the experience we were looking for, and tension started building. As it got to maximum tension, the relationship got stuck and we were frustrated as it seemed we were doing all the right things we read and learned about.

It took Laurie (the much smarter one on relationship matters) to see it and figure it out. We were at date night discussing this over a beautiful bottle of wine, trying to find the contradiction, when Laurie just said it plainly and clearly: "I am done with divide and conquer. It just separates us." Then she said, "Now we combine and conquer!"

Freud once said, "It seems to be my fate to discover the obvious." Well, when Laurie said it, it seemed so obvious. It is a contradiction to hold a value of staying deeply connected while simultaneously holding an operating premise that requires you to divide.

Let me make something very clear here. Divide and conquer, in and of itself is not wrong. It could be a perfect model for other people with other values. It was just wrong for us. As we go through the journey of this book together, this will gain more context, so I revisit this a bit at the end.

Your Values Are Yours Alone

It is important to note while engaging in this exercise that your values are *your values*. In other words, there are people who don't have the same standard for their love relationship that you have. There are people who don't hold the same values for fitness that you do. There is no right or wrong. There is only the matter of having values that you can consciously choose and make sure they align rather can conflict. It's a relative thing.

This is the crucial and critical first step in finding your stand to determine your brand. Now that we know how to identify contradictions and eliminate them, it's time to get into the nitty-gritty—a business-building sequence I've developed over the years that has created immense success, not only for myself, but for the entrepreneurs I've taught.

We'll discuss just what that process is in the next chapter.

Chapter Two

THE 5-*P* EXPANSION SEQUENCE

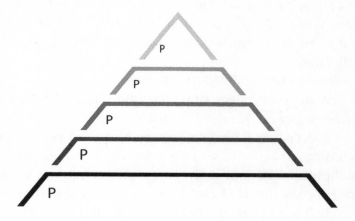

Many years ago, I was invited to speak to the entire student body at a university in the Atlanta area. The subject was how to create success in your life. It was a relatively short lecture, about forty-five minutes, and full of the typical bromides, platitudes, and catchphrases that sound great to inspire an audience. I ended the speech to a standing ovation. When I stepped down from the stage, there was a rush of people who wanted to speak with me individually. We speakers many times refer to this as "stage rush" and sometimes you have to exit backstage to avoid it, especially when there is a speaker right after you. Sometimes, however, you can step off and greet the people who want to share something, which I like to do when it is possible. I find it to be an opportunity to learn from my audience.

I was basking in the glow of attention when a student approached with pen and notebook in hand. He said, "Hey, that was a great speech, I really enjoyed what you had to say. Let me ask you, what are the steps to success?"

"Success is a mind-set," I told him. More platitudes. "It's all in your head. You have to develop the headspace for success." Mind you, it wasn't that I didn't believe that to be true, but it wasn't particularly helpful to say only that.

The student realized that as well.

"Yeah, yeah, I got that," he said. "But what are the actual steps I could take to create success?"

I didn't know how to answer him, and people were watching, so I gave him more of the high-level clichés and catchphrases I'd just delivered onstage—yet the student would not be deterred. He had a clear question in his mind.

"Again, I heard all that," he said. "But what I'm asking you is what is the step one, step two, step three in a sequence? What is the roadmap that I could follow?"

Admittedly, he'd caught me off guard, and I got to feeling quite awkward. He was asking me a *real* question—one to which I had no answer. I decided to be honest and tell him just that. I also said that because he was asking such a clear and important question, I would work on it and get back to him with a definitive answer within two weeks. He gave me his contact information, and I went to work on an answer to a real question, as compared to all the hype I had been spewing from the platform.

That experience was revelatory. Sure, I'd motivated people, but that student's question made me realize that I hadn't given them anything more than a hot tub experience. Nobody's life was going to change from what I'd shared with them. They'd be pumped up. They'd feed my ego by telling me how motivated they were after my presentation—but giving them a hot tub experience wasn't my purpose. That meant I needed to go to work on something that would give people—especially that student—a *pivotal* experience. I felt I owed him, particularly because his question was a pivotal experience for me.

As it turns out, that simple, clear question caused me to develop and answer that on a practical level translated into many millions of dollars in revenue for me and count-less amounts for those I had taught it to.

The concept I came up with is one that I've utilized now for more than twenty years to help me build my companies. It is still in its original form and application. I never found anything that needed modification—I only went deeper with it so I could understand why it works on a variety of levels. I've taught it as a process to thousands of doctors, business owners, executives, and entrepreneurs to successfully apply as a roadmap to their success.

That process is the 5-*P* Expansion Sequence.

The five *P*s are in order, meaning that the first *P* rep-resents the most fundamental concept. Emerging from that is the second *P*, then the third and fourth, with the fifth *P* serving as the final piece. The sequence is man-datory to the model. The cause and effect attributes are a nonnegotiable aspect of it, and as I'll point out, when people try to reverse the cause and effect relationship of these components, it leads to bad places.

First *P*: Philosophy

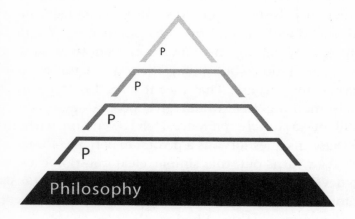

Right now, whether you know it or not, you have a philosophy. As I mentioned in the introduction, every human being on the planet has one—and so does every business. It is at the root of everything. Your philosophy defines how you think and how you apply your thinking as a tool for success. My intellectual mentor, Nathaniel Branden, taught me that you have no choice about the fact that you have or need a philosophy—your only choice is whether you've consciously defined it or not.

In the next chapter, we will do a deep dive into understanding the practical application of philosophy in business. What you need to know here is that for the 5-*P* Expansion Sequence, philosophy is the first and most foundational concept. There is nothing more fundamental in your life than how you think and how you use your thinking. It is at the basis of everything you do. Once you start to form concepts, you are in the realm of philosophy. It all starts there. It's ironic that most people view philosophy as some sort of impractical, abstract indulgence. The reality is that it is the *most* practical thing you and your business can hope to embrace.

Emerging out of your philosophy is your purpose.

Second *P*: Purpose

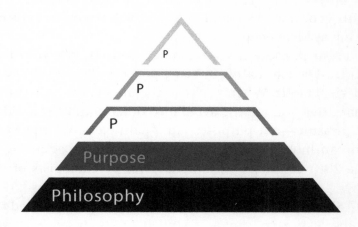

There have been many books and much discussion about the virtues of purpose—of being purpose-driven in your life and in your business. I've been speaking to this concept for quite some time. In fact, I started a business with a partner back in 1994 called On Purpose. I recognized, even then, how purpose was a motive force for the human experience, and how a clear purpose provided the rocket fuel to propel a business to success.

It's important to note that many gurus and consultants start with purpose as the foundation, but what they need to realize is the purpose doesn't drop from the sky. You don't get suddenly hit with the purpose stick (although sometimes it can feel that way). Purpose comes from something—and that something is your philosophy. It emerges out of the third branch of philosophy, ethics. Before you can get there, you have to develop the first two branches. Again, more on this in the next chapter.

What separates you from any other life form on Earth is that you can choose your purpose. A dog cannot choose its purpose in life—if it could, it probably wouldn't live with you. If a cow could choose, there would be no such thing as McDonald's.

Your purpose is your compass setting. It is your true north. The alternative to being purpose-driven is to be in survival mode. When you're in that mode, the only things that drive you are the avoidance of pain and the seeking of pleasure—not purpose. This "pain-pleasure" theory of human motivation was popularized in the beginning of the 20th century by the behavioral psychologists of the day.

Since that time, many self-help gurus have adopted the pain-pleasure concept and applied it to their seminars and teachings in personal development. Those gurus tell their audiences that they need to understand their behavior in terms of that principle, and they go on to give many examples that seem to ring true. There was always something in my gut that felt that it couldn't be that simplistic—not that it was entirely wrong, but that pleasure seeking and pain avoidance could not represent a complete characterization of what drives human beings. There was something dehumanizing about it.

Here's the thought experiment I take audiences through to help illustrate the distinctions and conclusions I've come to on this issue. Let's compare the direction you're leading your life or business to taking a walk through the woods. Suddenly, on your path you encounter a raging river. It would be quite painful to cross that river, so rather than continue in the direction you were going, you decide to take a left. As you continue on the path to the left, you encounter a large mountain. It would be very difficult to climb, so you turn again to avoid it. This path seems clearer for a good while and you feel some relief. All is well and good until you discover that the farther you travel in that direction, the weather becomes cold and rainy and it's getting worse. Obviously, you'd rather avoid the pain of that weather, so you change directions yet again, heading south where the climate is warmer.

In essence, you're avoiding the pain that ends up in front of you, hoping to find pleasure by some chance, and now you—and your business—are wandering aimlessly, seeking pleasure and avoiding pain.

Now let's look at an alternate scenario. Let's imagine that you have a clear purpose for your business, and that purpose can be dialed into a compass as true north. The compass heading leads you to the river with those rough rapids, and while you realize it will be painful and maybe even a bit risky to cross it, the alternative is to make a turn and lose your purpose, your true north. So instead, your compass directs you to cross the river. Your purpose demands that you steel yourself for the pain and get yourself to the other side.

Now you come to that big, daunting mountain, and the mountain range extends such that there is no easy way or shortcut around it. Once again, you collect your energy and resolve and you climb it, because your purpose-driven compass directs you that way. You keep moving, and when the cold and rain hit, you pull up your hood, bundle up, and forge on through the tough weather.

What also happens when you continue your journey in the direction of your purpose is that eventually, instead of another set of raging waters, you encounter a serene reflecting pond. You take a moment to sit there and reflect in pleasure about your journey.

Then you continue on, and gone are the mountains you had to summit. Now there is a vast green field of soft grass. You decide to take off your shoes and feel the joy of the grass under your feet as you proceed with your walk.

Now the sun is out warming you. You peel off a couple of layers, lift your chin, and smile broadly as the sun hits your face and warms your being.

You see, when you are purpose-driven on your journey, sometimes there is pain, sometimes there is pleasure, but your constant and most important companion is *purpose*.

Pain and pleasure will always come and go on an alternating basis. That is the way it is supposed to be. For me, aesthetically, there is a beauty in this—something humanizing. When I consider the pain-pleasure model of human motivation, I find it dehumanizing. Remember, what makes human beings different than every other form of animal on the planet is that we can "choose" a purpose. We can abstractly consider it. When we are in survival mode—when we don't have a clear purpose that drives us—then we are living a subhuman experience, like any other animal whose innate program is to survive.

In order to know the full human experience, and in order for your business to be something of consequence that can make an impact in this world, you and everyone involved in your business must be aligned and purpose-driven. When there is clarity as to why the business exists and you can align every stakeholder in it, you now have the rocket fuel to propel you to ever greater heights.

Philosophy and purpose are causes in the sequence. The next three *P*s are effects.

Third *P*: Psychology

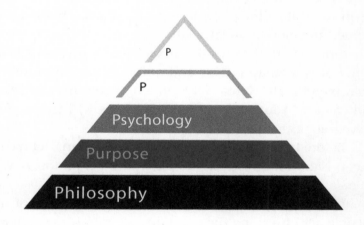

This is an area where I strongly feel the self-help gurus get wrong. Often, they look at psychology and psychological states as a cause, when the reality is, they are effects. Emotions, for the most part, are not primaries, they are secondaries. When you are someone who is constantly driven by manipulating your emotional states as a primary driver to try to create success, you turn yourself into a self-help junkie.

Before I developed the 5-*P* Expansion Sequence, all I gave that audience of college students I mentioned earlier was clichés and platitudes. The effects of that hot tub experience would wear off in a day or two, changing the lives of no one. That is the nature of manipulating psycho-emotional states without changing an underlying philosophy to support them.

This is not to say that psychology and psycho-emotional states aren't important. If they weren't, they wouldn't be part of this sequence. Further, I can tell you that creating temporary heightened psychological states for performance can be very useful—but it is also very fleeting. It can help deal with an immediate goal or crisis but doesn't help long-term to create a life or a successful business. That requires something more foundational.

Once again, the mistakes made around psychology are when it is seen as a cause and not an effect. My intellectual mentor, Dr. Nathaniel Branden, made this clarifying statement: "Your philosophical premises will shape your psychological experiences."

Before I give an example of what this means, let me be clear: I am not advocating for any political philosophy. It is meant solely to be illustrative of the concept.

Let's say there are three people in a room. Two of the people are observing the third engaging in some activity. One of the observers is quite liberal in their economic philosophy, while the other is staunchly conservative. Between the two of them, they are watching the third who is the country's leader signing a new law into existence that is going to radically increase the taxes on higher income producers and redistribute that wealth.

What do you think the emotional experience of the economically liberal-minded person is going to be? Obviously, this person will be extremely happy with what they're observing. They will be smiling. They will feel like celebrating. Life will feel "right."

On the other hand, what would you suppose the psycho-emotional experience of the conservative-leaning observer will be? As you could imagine, this person will be angry. They'll feel despair—maybe even depressed and frustrated. Life will feel "wrong."

How is it that two grown individuals who are simultaneously and accurately observing the exact same thing at the exact same time have diametrically opposed psycho-emotional experiences? They both see the situation for exactly what it is, they both fully understand the nature of what is happening, yet they are having completely opposite emotional experiences. What causes the difference?

Their *philosophy*. Their philosophical premises dictate their psycho-emotional experiences. Philosophy is the primary, the cause. Emotions are the secondaries, or the effect.

To recap, it is important to understand that from your philosophy emerges your values and purpose, and these two things will dictate your psycho-emotional experiences in the world. To try only to manipulate your psycho-emotional states without giving any thought or regard to your fundamental philosophy is short-lived and unsustainable. You will constantly be dragged back into the states that your philosophical values dictate.

Understanding this becomes a critical tool when you are experiencing "mixed emotions," or conflicting emotions where you feel stuck about a decision—whether it be about personal relationships or a business issue. Those emotions are a sign of contradictions in your basic philosophy and its values. The way to resolve those mixed emotions is by identifying those contradictions and aligning them, much in the ways we discussed in the previous chapter.

Emotional states are critical to achievement. As a two-time national karate champion, I can speak quite clearly to what it takes to put yourself in a heightened state of performance to go out and be successful—in my case, success meant winning tournaments. Even though I personally appreciate how useful emotional-state management can be, I also know that when you're dealing with psychological states as a primary cause to create your next level of success, you're a step away from the tragedy of jumping on the self-help junkie merry-go-round.

It is for this reason that we'll spend the entire next chapter understanding philosophy as the cause, and psychology as the effect.

Fourth *P*: Procedure

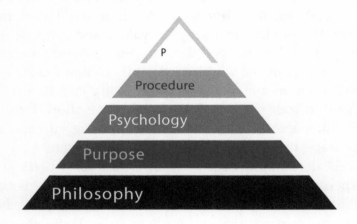

I've spent a lot of time and money reading books, listening to podcasts, hiring consultants, and going to seminars on business growth and development. Many of these are targeted toward teaching you new and better and well-tested procedures. This relates to all dimensions of the business—sales and marketing, human resources, operations, accounting, you name it. All sustainable businesses must have procedures in place for every function of the business.

The dirty little secret is, procedures alone don't create success.

I know, I know, you're saying, "But the new webinar selling the latest social media strategies guarantees me that I will grow my revenue by 50 percent or more or my money back!" However, take a look at the fine print where it states "results may vary." Ever wonder why they need to say that? The reason is because results *will* vary. It's a fact. No speculation there. Ah, but this far into the chapter, by now you should understand clearly why results will vary.

Because it is not the procedure that gets the result.

Keeping in line with the 5-*P* model, you now understand that your procedures manage the effects of what your philosophy and your purpose create. Philosophy and purpose are the motive force—the great cause. It's not the procedures that get the results—it's the person or the business performing the procedure that gets the result.

Please understand, I am *not* saying that procedures are unimportant. They are critically important. Heck, they are one of the 5 *P*s; however, procedures that are in contradiction with the philosophy and purpose of the business will keep you from getting across the finish line of success. They become a limiting factor. So, if your procedures are currently contradicting your philosophy and purpose, then by getting alignment there, you would have a great breakthrough. However, if you are a, let's say, $2 million per year small business, and you learn some better procedures, but nothing that creates more alignment or clarity along the 5 *P*s, then what happens is you just get better at generating $2 million per year.

Here's a thought experiment. Let's say that I'm teaching a seminar on marketing strategies. I have ten business owners in front of me with their marketing directors, all there to learn a new social media strategy or digital marketing technique that involves generating traffic and converting it into business. Let's say I tested this in my own business, liked what I saw, and now I want to share it with these seminar attendees. Imagine that I teach it to all of them and they all learn it in the exact same manner. They leave the seminar excited, go back to their companies, and they all apply the material in the exact same way that I presented it. They're all going to get the same result, right?

Wrong. It's not the procedure that gets the result; it's "who" the person or company is that is doing the procedure that gets the result.

It is the "who" before the "do"—and the "who" is defined by philosophy and purpose.

What happens far too often is that people get clarity about their philosophy and purpose and then they are psychologically aligned. Everything starts moving, but then—*BAM*—their procedures come in conflict with those elements and it's like hitting a brick wall with a sign on it that says, *"Your growth stops here."*

Procedures that have *big* contradictions to the business purpose are easy to spot and more often than not get corrected. As the old saying goes, it's not the red flags that get you—it's the yellow flags that insidiously take you down. Ever hire someone that you were excited about, but there was a little attitude or behavior that was off? Maybe you decided to overlook and rationalize it by saying things to yourself like, *Oh, really smart people are quirky. It's just a package deal.* Then months or more go by and those "little quirks" start to disrupt and degenerate the business and its culture. This applies to affiliates, vendors, and any other people who are involved with your business. Their values aren't aligned, you make excuses for it, and it haunts you later.

I never worry about red flags. It's an easy "no"—but those yellow flags will mess you up.

Incidentally, it goes without saying that this very much applies to personal relationships, too. When you start dating and you ignore yellow flags, I see pain in your future. Let me give you an example from my own career.

What's critical to witness in this example is the connection among philosophical premise, purpose, procedure, and outcome. My original chiropractic practice had a purpose that was built on the fundamental philosophy of the profession. It's really beautiful in its power and simplicity. In short, the chiropractic premise holds that the body is intelligent, self-healing and self-regulating, and that the nervous system is the master controller coordinating all the functions of the body. Logically, if you interfere with nervous system function, you interfere with the ability of the body to heal and regulate. Stress in your life, beyond what your body can naturally adapt to, will compromise your nervous system function, which alters the tone of the muscles around your spine, leading to what chiropractors describe as subluxations (misaligned spinal segments). In other words, spinal bones are out of their normal and healthy position, causing compromise in neural function.

Since we literally live our lives through our nervous systems, uncorrected, this can lead to health challenges— some of them serious. On the flip side, when subluxations are corrected with chiropractic adjustments, people can have incredible health breakthroughs. I've witnessed it thousands of times. Also, it is important to understand in this example is that in most cases, correcting these spinal misalignments is a process over time. It doesn't just happen in a few visits.

Given this backdrop, the purpose of my business was to acknowledge the fact that there was an urgent problem in our community where people were overstressed, overmedicated, and becoming increasingly sicker. My practice existed to take radical action in educating the community about this predicament and the chiropractic solution to it, as well as to provide the care necessary to restore and maintain their health.

Most people who came to my office had some sort of back or neck pain and were seeking relief, which was limited care. My intention would be not only to relieve their pain, but to adjust and correct their subluxations patterns so that they could experience higher levels of health, even after the pain was gone. Basically, people came in thinking they had a back problem when what they really had was a health problem. Therefore the goal was to give my patients lifetime family wellness care, not just relief from pain.

The chiropractic philosophy toward health and how to achieve it is a unique and powerful thing. Unfortunately, there are many chiropractors who don't practice based on this philosophy. It's a good example of how there can be two people who by all outward appearances seem to be in the same business called chiropractic practice, but they can have very different philosophies that drive their business. Therefore, they have a different purpose, different psychology, and should absolutely have different procedures. They are not at all in the same business, even though their signs might say the same thing.

After a couple of years in practice, I realized a frustration. I was having trouble getting people to continue care for correction of their subluxations. They would typically quit once their pain was relieved. This was evidence to me that there was a contradiction somewhere and I had to find it. The amount of personal energy it was taking me to hold up my practice was exhausting. I wanted to grow it, but there was no way for me to do it if I had to increase my energy output proportionately. Even though I didn't have the 5-*P* model at the time, I knew enough to go back to my philosophy and try to figure it out from there.

After some deep evaluation, I had a eureka moment. The contradiction was in my procedures. When I gave patients my doctor's report explaining my findings, I did it all through the lens of the philosophy of chiropractic as I explained it above. This led to the purpose of the practice—why it existed, what goals I set out for the patients, and what care plans I recommended. However, many of my exam procedures were not aimed at finding subluxations and monitoring their correction. They were steeped in traditional medical orthopedic and neurological evaluations. These tests were largely designed to assess areas of pain in the body, to rate that pain, and identify the source of it. These tests may have had some limited use but should not have been at the core of my exam procedure. Hence, aspects of my procedures were in contradiction with my philosophy and purpose.

The result of that procedural contradiction was that I limited the size of my business and how far I could take it. To put it in tough terms, *I was selling a product I was not certain I was delivering.* In fact, recognizing this is what led me to co-develop new diagnostic technology with Dr. Christopher Kent, and begin my diagnostic technology business—so that I could remove a contradiction within my own practice. My goal was to create an examination procedure that would align with the philosophy and purpose of my practice, and it was clear to me that if I were having this problem, so were thousands and thousands of my colleagues. Identifying that contradiction for myself and others is how that business was born. After twenty-three years, by the time I exited that business we had over eight thousand clients on six continents. When I say applied philosophy is practical, I mean *very* practical.

Fifth *P*: Prosperity

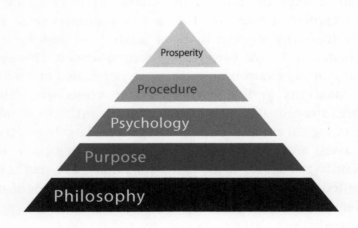

Once you have aligned your philosophy, purpose, psychology, and procedures, the ultimate effect is prosperity.

The most important thing to know is that prosperity is the ultimate effect of who you are—*not the cause.* If you get this upside down, you will constantly find yourself in survival mode, always struggling in an endless grab for prosperity—and you'll never find it. I've seen this light bulb go off after teaching this to tens of thousands of people. They have quite literally had a pivotal experience in front of me, where they recognize that for their entire career, the pyramid of their five *P*s has been upside down. The day they wake up to the fact that it needs to be right-side up is the day they have a breakthrough that gets them where they need to be. When one starts with the dream to make a lot of money in business and is willing to work their tail off doing it, it's easy to understand how they unwittingly start their whole thinking process looking through the lens of "prosperity as a cause." The mistake is *not* understanding that prosperity as a cause, rarely results in, well, prosperity. They may be able to do well temporarily, but it is not sustainable.

The better perspective is to figure out the philosophy and purpose and have that result in prosperity. If the purpose is strong, no amount of money will buy you out of it (examples of this to follow). How do you know if you are on purpose? *You start to see money as a means to expand the range of your purpose*, as compared to a way to stop working.

I have a longtime dear friend named Lee Brody. He was the lead engineer on our diagnostic technology and the co-inventor on my patents. He is one of the smartest people I've ever met and I am continually awestruck by his strategic abilities as a CEO. One time we were on the phone discussing how our kids are growing up and how they were trying to figure out what they wanted "to do for a living." Lee said to me, a better question to ask them is, "What problem do you want to solve?" Brilliant. When people think about doing something for a living, it leads them to asking, "How much money can I make doing that?" However, if they are looking at spending their days solving a problem, they now are thinking in terms of having a purpose. When you have a clear purpose and play to your strengths in actualizing it (and that part is critical!), then the money will come.

How do you know if you are on purpose? *You start to see money as a means to expand the range of your purpose*, as compared to a way to stop working.

One of the docuseries we made for Revealed Films was entitled, *Money Revealed*. It was our most successful project to date and the feedback was startlingly positive. Here is the write-up we did for it, stating its core values, vision, and Statement of Purpose. I do this as a first step for every project.

Money Revealed Core Values

- Financial Freedom
- Financial Wisdom
- Financial Innovation
- Financial Security
- Conscious Capitalism
- Self-Reliance
- Enlightenment

Vision

To make financial illiteracy a thing of the past.

Statement of Purpose

There is an urgent problem in our culture where education, understanding, and perspectives relative to money are warped, misinformed, and in many cases nonexistent. People can work hard and generate significant income for decades and still find themselves toward the end of their careers in debt and worried with no real financial strategy to carry them comfortably through the rest of their lives.

Money Revealed exists to be a beacon of light, exposing hidden truths, wisdom, and innovations that will transform the financial destiny of millions of people resulting in security, freedom, and a legacy that otherwise would not be possible.

One of the celebrity experts I interviewed for *Money Revealed* was Robert Kiyosaki, and it was an experience I will never forget.

Robert is intelligent, animated, completely unabashed, and the depth of his wisdom was readily apparent. As he told his famous story contrasting the philosophy of his poor dad with his friend's rich dad, he would make statements like, "School prepares you to have a job and I didn't want a job! I wanted to be rich!" At first you might interpret this to mean that all he cared about was making money, but this was not even close to being true. As a matter of fact, one of the most poignant moments of the interview was when he teared up, lamenting the fact that many young and talented people who wanted to work with him and do deals only cared about making money.

To paraphrase it a bit, he said they had no soul. It broke his heart to the point of tears. To Robert Kiyosaki, and many others like him—like Whole Foods Market co-founder and CEO John Mackey, whom I also interviewed for *Money Revealed*—making money was a *spiritual* experience. There was a purpose behind it. Creating lots of jobs, enriching the lives of all stakeholders, value-creating on the large scale, and generating lots of money—these were moral virtues.

It wasn't so much that these "young bucks" who just wanted to make money were immoral. They were *amoral*. They had no purpose or spirit that motivated them. They just wanted to make money, and the thought of this brought tears to the producer who has a purpose.

How about some extreme examples of prosperity being the ultimate effect and not a cause? For many years, Bill Gates (love him or hate him) was the wealthiest man in the world. On March 13, 1986, when Microsoft went public, he was thirty years old and worth $350 million. Now if prosperity is your cause and not your effect, and you're worth that much money—particularly in that year—how many more days would you have to go to work? None. Yet, not only did he continue to keep working, he kept on until his net worth was $50 *billion*—an inconceivable amount of personal wealth. Even then, Gates went to work every day.

His prosperity was the effect of who he was, not the cause. As a matter of fact, while Gates was the richest man in the world, he didn't continue on as CEO of the company—he stayed on as Microsoft's chief software architect, because that was his purpose all along. That's how he got his start. There was no amount of money that could buy him out of the work that was his purpose. If $50 billion wasn't going to do it, nothing would have.

Consider Michael Jordan. How many multimillion-dollar Nike contracts do you need before you don't need to play basketball anymore? Recently, it was estimated that Jordan was netting, on average, $40 million per year. While he was playing and winning championships, he had extraordinary amounts of endorsement income, as well as his salary. His playing salary over the course of his career is estimated at $90 million (this was in the '80s!). At the time of this writing, Jordan's net worth is $1.9 billion. When Jordan retired from basketball, some estimated his net worth to be approximately $400 million–$500 million. There was no amount of money that could buy him off the court. In fact, he retired and came back two years later, only to give his entire annual salary to the 9/11 charities. His purpose, for as long as he physically could, was to play the game. The prosperity he created was the effect of that purpose. When he couldn't play anymore? He bought a basketball team.

How many more bad movies does Sylvester Stallone have to make? (I'm *totally* kidding; I'm an enthusiastic *Rocky* fan!) Stallone has amassed immense wealth, yet he continues to star in and produce movies. Before the first *Rocky* was made, Stallone was a starving actor and writer, living in a flophouse for $26 a week sharing a floor with ten people you don't know and don't want to know. At that time, he couldn't even, as he put it, "get casted as an Italian." He wrote *Rocky* and was offered $360,000 for the script, which, for the time period in the 1970s, was a very large sum of money, especially for an unemployed actor living in such conditions.

Stallone refused. He knew it was his purpose to play Rocky in the film he had written. Most people, particularly in that mode of survival, would have taken the money and moved on to the next thing. Stallone, however, was clear in his purpose. There was no amount of money he would take to give up playing that role. Because purpose was his cause, prosperity was his effect. He is now one of the most successful people in the history of Hollywood.

Understanding the sequence of how you move from philosophy to prosperity is crucial. It doesn't matter if you're a solopreneur or if you're in a Fortune 100 company—these rules always apply.

As you can probably see by now, none of this is possible unless you can understand your philosophy at a deep level—so let's read on and tackle that in the next chapter.

Chapter Three

UNLEASHING THE POWER OF PHILOSOPHY

Let's return to my bicycle accident in New York City.

I mentioned that while I had been recovering, I had nothing but time on my hands, so I became a voracious reader. Through my reading, I began to identify things that I'd always felt very deeply but had never been able to put into words. By the time I had finished *The Fountainhead*, not only was the drama of the story something I found quite intriguing, but I had a new clarity in my way of thinking about and seeing the world. I wanted more.

I desperately needed an integrated view of existence, and that is what philosophy can give you.

Ayn Rand was, and still is, a very polarizing figure. Love her or hate her, she made some profound statements and had a massive impact. Even if you don't agree with all of Rand's views, I don't think there is any argument about her use of philosophy as a tool for success. It was Rand who, in my opinion, best championed the critical and practical application of philosophy in life.

For a long period of time, Ayn Rand had an intellectual heir who helped spread her philosophy, a psychotherapist named Dr. Nathaniel Branden. I studied Dr. Branden's work and knew it well. Nathaniel Branden was perhaps the number one person in the world I wanted to meet.

You've heard me use the phrase "pivotal experience." Many years ago, I experienced yet another one for myself. There was a philosophy symposium being held in New York City, and Dr. Branden was one of the presenters. I was extremely excited to hear the man lecture live, as well as thrilled at the prospect of potentially meeting him.

It's important to note that even longer before this moment, Rand and Branden had had an acrimonious split that led to Branden being excommunicated from her inner circle. That story became a dramatic book in and of itself, written by Dr. Branden, titled *My Years with Ayn Rand*—a book that to me was so riveting I read it in a day and a half.

Branden accomplished something pivotal in Rand's philosophical movement—he commercialized and taught the practical applications of her philosophy, called "Objectivism," through his own Nathaniel Branden Institute. I was able to acquire all of the audio recordings of those series of presentations on philosophy, its branches, and the practical applications of philosophy in life—dozens of hours of content in all. Any spare minute I had went to listening to those recordings repeatedly. I learned all of the branches, understood the applications, began utilizing them in my life, and started teaching them to others.

In my mind, the fundamental premise as to why philosophy is such a practical tool for success is simply, to paraphrase Rand, that contradictions lead to destruction. Said another way—and as we said previously in this book—contradictions in your basic philosophical premises will lead to destruction, and the amount of destruction is relative to the level of that contradiction. It's as simple as that, and as difficult as that.

It is simple to say that if you have contradictions, it will lead to aspects of your life or business that won't work or begin to collapse, and that the more glaring the contradictions, the bigger the difficulties or destruction will be. No one is completely contradiction-free. We can always identify contradictions and remove them. As we do, we evolve to higher levels of effectiveness in our lives and in our businesses. That, however, can be the difficult part.

Later in this book, we have an entire chapter on brand purity, and one of the ways to achieve that purity is by removing contradictions in your business. Consider that a teaser for now.

Meanwhile, let's return to the symposium.

I sat in Dr. Branden's class and was awed by how precise his thinking and language were—and how stimulating his ideas were. After his presentation was complete, I walked to the front of the room to meet him personally. I speak with no hyperbole when I tell you that there was an immediate connection. As soon as we shook hands, we began speaking as if we'd known each other for years. We exchanged business cards and I asked him if he would come speak at some of the programs I held. He gladly accepted.

This was the start of an extraordinary relationship that lasted for many years. We became close friends. Dr. Branden became my intellectual mentor and we had what he would characterize spiritually as a father-and-son relationship. Nathaniel had no children, so another dear friend Jon Butcher and I became his "adopted children." In fact, I own a first edition *Atlas Shrugged* that he signed, as his name is in the dedication of the book, and he inscribed it, "To my adopted son."

Nathaniel was best known for his work on self-esteem. His seminal book on the subject was *The Six Pillars of Self-Esteem*. As I mentioned earlier, I used to run immersion programs—what some people might refer to as boot camps—that were intensive, four-day trainings in the mountains of Colorado.

What I had realized after being in diagnostic tech business after seven years was that it wasn't the technology that was getting the result in my clients' offices—it was the person using it that got the result. I recognized that in order for people to upgrade their success in a significant way, we needed to work on the "who" before we worked on the "how." That's where Nathaniel's work came into play. The name of the boot camp was Total Solution. On day two, Nathaniel would teach an entire workshop on the six pillars of self-esteem, and it was amazingly transformative for the group.

However, the first evening of the program opened with my philosophy lecture, which laid out the foundation for the entire program. Depending on the group, the presentation would take anywhere from four to six hours to get through. The great thing about the immersion program is that we were far away from civilization. We bussed them in, and they weren't leaving till we bussed them out. They weren't going anywhere. If I had to go to one or two o'clock in the morning to get the job done, then I did that.

On one particular occasion, Nathaniel came and sat in on my presentation. His piercing blue eyes were laser-focused on me the entire time, and it actually started to make me a little uncomfortable. His intensity and concentration as I presented the material that I originally learned from him was more than a bit unnerving. Nonetheless, I got into my zone and kept at it. Once I completed the presentation, right around midnight, I released the group to go back to their rooms and get some sleep. Nathaniel stood up, walked straight over to me, and grabbed both of my shoulders. His shock of silver hair atop his head, his chin down, he stared with those blue eyes into mine and said, "I need you to listen to me right now."

He had my attention.

He squeezed my shoulders and said, "What Rand once gave to me, I now give to you."

People often talk about moments in their lives that took their breath away. This was one of those moments for me. I understood the full range and impact of what he was trying to communicate to me. He, for many years, was the intellectual heir to Ayn Rand. He promulgated her material in the world like no one else did. He was the person who translated the philosophy that was in her fictional works and turned it into a practical application for human life on planet Earth. Before I ever met him, he was the one who helped me understand the power of the practical application of philosophy to humanity. I took it further and developed it into the practical application of philosophy in business.

And he had just passed the torch to me.

Thinking back on the moment is still somewhat mind-numbing. Nathaniel was an unusual genius, although he hated it when I called him that. Once he said to me,

"Would you please stop referring to me as a genius? I am not a genius!" I replied by reviewing his intellectual achievements over the span of many decades. He smiled and said, "Okay, you can refer to me as such."

I don't use the word *genius* too often, but Nathaniel was unequivocally that and more. He passed some years ago, and I was honored and grateful to be able to give a eulogy at his memorial service. There is no way I could ever adequately describe the value that he added to my life, and the joy that our friendship brought. It is my hope that in some small way, I can honor him with the subject matter that I'll share with you in this chapter.

You Have a Philosophy

Whether you know it or not, the business—or businesses—that you're involved with have a philosophy. Everyone and every business has a philosophy. The only question is: Have you defined it in a conscious manner? Have you let it serve as the foundation from which to build your business?

There are these motive forces in your life or business that are either tearing it apart or driving it toward the next level of effectiveness.

I reiterate this because it is important to drill this notion into your brain. Why is it important that you know your philosophy, and that it's defined in as clear a way as possible? As I described earlier, when you have contradictions in your basic philosophical premises, the only possible result is destruction.

When I highlighted maximum tension earlier, I pointed to contradictions in the driving forces of your life. When I used the phrase "philosophical premises" in the last chapter, I was defining premises as belief elements that drive your thoughts and actions, whether you know it or not. *There are these motive forces in your life or business that are either tearing it apart or driving it toward the next level of effectiveness.*

The point here is to have a structure—a framework from which you can think and act. The genius of the Nathaniel Branden Institute, where he taught the practical application of philosophy, was the fact that you can break philosophy down into five branches and then align them in a sequence that will take you from start to finish through the entire understanding of philosophy and how to apply it to your life and business.

We'll review those branches in a moment—but first, let's examine some examples of contradictions at work.

Many years ago, when McDonald's fast-food restaurants were new and the idea of fast food was exploding, there was another restaurant that came on the scene called Chutes. I know, you never heard of it—and there's a reason why. I studied this business case years ago and can't even find it anywhere online today. It was born out of a group of investors who were looking at the success of McDonald's and realized that fast food was a huge future industry in America. So, this group of skilled and intelligent people got together, formed their capital, and decided that they were going to be the restaurant to outperform McDonald's by getting creative and delivering food faster than McDonald's did.

They devised a pneumatic system of delivery through tubes—hence the name Chutes—so the food could be delivered to the customer, in this novel way, even faster. They brought together engineers, business operators, financiers—all the brightest people they could find to create the foundation for a successful franchise. They were all excited about the prospect of being able to beat McDonald's at their own game—and as fate would have it, they failed miserably.

Why? Why did these very smart and skilled people who were well funded and who executed on their plan fail in their venture?

Because they had a faulty premise—a fundamental contradiction.

In general terms, I like to break contradictions down into two broad categories—external, or contradictions with reality, and internal, or contradictions with self.

External contradictions are when you have operating premises about how things really are, and you are wrong about it. This meant that when you are having challenges, perhaps you are making assumptions about what's true that are inaccurate. We are constantly struggling and striving in business to assess reality. Some aspects of reality are constant, like gravity. Some aspects of reality are fluid, like consumer and marketplace behavior. Whether something is constant or fluid, it's essential to know what's true, and the degree that you are wrong about this is the degree of destruction you'll experience relative to it. The contradiction with the example of Chutes is an external contradiction—a contradiction with reality.

Internal contradictions are more insidious because they are related to self-deception and dissonance. In most cases, the self-deception is totally unconscious. Hence, it makes it very tricky to try to navigate these waters and correct these contradictions. For businesses or individuals that decide that they want to start sorting this out, as we start to unpack our philosophy, we see it starts to look like a junk heap. This is actually really good news, because you have to identify the junk heap before you can clean it up. Most people readily get and to some degree apply the concept of external contradictions. Very few people ever wake up to the concept of internal contradictions.

As for Chutes, their premise?

Their premise was that the reason people flocked to McDonald's was because they wanted their food *fast*. What they found out in hindsight was the reason people actually went to McDonald's in droves was that they liked the *taste* of the food, and that getting it fast was a bonus. Chutes thought that by beating McDonald's at the speed game, they would beat them in the marketplace. That premise was wrong and proved to be fatal to their business. They had a contradiction in their basic premise, and it was a high level of external contradiction—and their amount of destruction—which was total, was relative to that level of contradiction.

A number of my business activities have been and continue to be in the healthcare arena. As you might have deduced from the introduction, much of my work lies in healthcare activism, changing minds to a higher truth about health and how it is properly achieved. I'm someone who believes that business activism can and should be profitable. How is one who wishes to change the world through activism going to be able to do that if they're broke?

I'm going to share something with you that might cause you to disagree with me, and that's okay. My point here is not to get you to agree with me—it's to give you further understanding as to how contradictions lead to destruction. Keep that in mind.

According to an article published in *Fortune*, the cost of healthcare in 2018 in the United States hit an astronomical $3.65 trillion. This amount is larger than the GDPs of such countries as Brazil, the U.K., and Canada. It's inconceivable. This spending represents $11,212 per person—that's every man, woman, and child in the United States! This is unsustainable if it continues along on its current trajectory. If we were all getting healthier and becoming more productive as a culture, I could see this as a somewhat sound investment, although there would still need to be some cost reduction. Quite the opposite is true, however. We are getting sicker and sicker, with explosive amounts of disease, disability, autoimmune disorders, autism, and other illnesses that are destroying many families, along with the foundation and productivity of our country.

In fact, the U.S. spends more money per capita than any other country in the world, but somewhat embarrassingly, various rankings show a pitiful return on investment. For example, a study published in May 2018 in the *Lancet*, a highly regarded peer-reviewed research journal, put the United States at number 29 in the world. Yes, Greece, Malta, and several other surprising countries ranked better.

As a side note, I can tell you that one can really get into the weeds when it comes to trying to rank countries on such things. The data and variables are quite complex and certainly not within the scope of this book.

This example presents one of the biggest contradictions I can conceive of. The reason we have this healthcare and economic catastrophe on our hands is because we call medicine *healthcare*. Medicine, the conventional practice of it, is *not* healthcare. It is *sick* care. When you take sick care and give it to a culture as healthcare, you end up with a sick society. This is why we spend over

$3.5 trillion a year and continue getting sicker every year. Understand that I am not anti-medicine. I believe medicine saves lives every single day. I'm simply stating that it is *not* healthcare. On a cultural level, applying it as *healthcare* is a huge contradiction, and the level of destruction it's creating is unparalleled.

The cause of this problem is not economic. It's philosophical. Until we fix the philosophical contradiction, we will never gain control of the economic destruction, which is an effect and not a cause.

How to Apply *Your* Philosophy

You might be asking at this point: How do I organize my philosophy, identify contradictions, and remove them? In order to answer that, I'm going to introduce you to the branches of philosophy and tell you how to apply them. There is some heavy lifting here, but I promise you it is worth it.

I need to make a strong point here. Many academic philosophers are going to disagree with much of what I propose. They will say that my descriptions and applications are not traditional—maybe even inaccurate to a degree. Let me state in no uncertain terms—I am *not* an academic philosopher. I don't have, nor care to have, an academic degree in philosophy. When it comes to philosophy, I am more of a "street philosopher," or as some like to say in my introductions, a philosopher-entrepreneur. So, for any academics who want to critique my use of applied philosophy for business and personal development, I ask that you keep this in mind.

It's important to note that there is a scaling phenomenon with applied philosophy. It is utilized on the widest imaginable aspects of your life and business, literally assessing the very purpose of its existence, and it can also be directed at the smallest procedure or process within your life or business.

This brings to mind the adage: How do you eat an elephant? One bite at a time. Let me share that applying philosophy to my life and businesses started having real impact on day one (as I think you'll soon discover), but after over two decades of doing so, I am still expanding my understanding of it and have a long way to go. This rabbit hole runs deep—very deep. All this to say, enjoy this as a journey, otherwise you'll resent it by being frustrated that you haven't arrived at a destination.

When Branden and Rand collaborated on this topic, they created what I believe is a brilliant sequence of the five branches and their practical application. The branches in sequence are:

- Metaphysics—your view of the nature of reality
- Epistemology—your theory of knowledge
- Ethics—provides human beings (or businesses) with a code of values, and therefore a guide to actions
- Politics—takes ethical values and applies them to social functions
- Aesthetics—the artistic representation of your philosophical views

My aim here is to walk you through these five branches, how they sequentially relate to each other, thereby giving you a framework from which to process your thinking.

This may sound like heavy intellectual stuff, and to an extent, that's true. What I can tell you is that I've taught this to tens of thousands of people worldwide, and when it clicks, not only do they utilize it themselves, but I find them teaching it to their children. Once you wrap your head around it, there is a sort of "far-side simplicity" that takes hold. In fact, I've created a program called the Philosophy Formula, and this formula is something I now wish to share with you.

There's a breakthrough here if you're willing to engage your mind, right now. With live audiences, I found that the breakthrough occurs right after the height of mental frustration. This mode of thinking is different, so a bit of chaos and confusion accompanies the destabilization of old thinking patterns, then they reorganize into something that performs on a higher level.

So, dial up your concentration a bit and let's do this.

The Philosophy Formula

Below is the actual "formula" that pulls it all together.

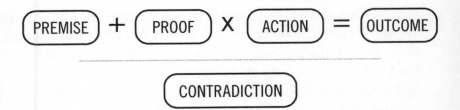

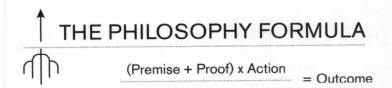

Let's take a tour of the branches and learn to apply them.

Branch 1: Metaphysics

Metaphysics is defined as your view of the nature of reality—your view of the nature of the universe. In essence, metaphysics asks the questions: Where am I? What is the nature of this place? What are the facts of reality?

Many times, when we hear the term metaphysics, we think about things like the New Age movement and mysticism. Although these are perspectives in metaphysics, they are not categorically metaphysics. There are a multitude of views in metaphysics.

You have certain views of reality that you hold, and these are driving your choices and actions whether you know it or not. Your business holds various views as well. Our story about Chutes demonstrated that they held a view of reality that said that the primary motivator for customers was that people wanted their food quickly. This was in contradiction to the reality of the situation, which is why their business didn't work.

Further, certain metaphysical premises—views of reality—may have been instilled in you by your "mothers, fathers, teachers, and preachers." Maybe you heard things like, "succeeding in business is a matter of luck," "don't trust anyone, it's a dog-eat-dog world," "you shouldn't bite off more than you can chew," "you shouldn't try to be something you're not," "rich people are thieves," "it's a man's world," or one I gave earlier, "success requires sacrifice."

We are all carrying this stuff around and unless we start to consciously identify our metaphysical premises and delete the ones that don't serve us and adopt the ones that do, we are doomed to mediocrity—and so are our businesses.

Branch 2: Epistemology

Epistemology is the theory of knowledge, and it asks the questions: How do I know? What are my rules of evidence? If you take a metaphysical premise like "success requires sacrifice," now we need to ask, "How do I know this? What is the evidence that supports it?"

"How do I know?" can be a powerful question. I've seen it change people's lives on the spot. They realized they've adopted foundational beliefs without ever questioning their validity. For example, you may have heard many times and adopted the premise, "It is better to give than receive." Have you ever asked, "How do I know this? What evidence is there that this is true?" By the way, I am not saying it is not true, but I can tell you that there is a deep amount of thinking and lots of trails to follow before you can validate or invalidate such a statement. Now you might say, "Well, that's just abstract stuff and really doesn't have any practicality for my daily life."

You couldn't be more wrong.

When we are looking at generalized personal premises, perhaps in the quest of clarifying our identity and further, if we are looking to understand the soul of our business (something we dig deep into in subsequent chapters), asking the questions, "Why do I believe it?" or "How do I know it?" become somewhat of a right-brained spiritual quest.

However, when it comes to detailed business management, as you'll see below, it is more of a left-brained, didactic exercise. The soul-searching side of epistemology, to me, is a priority before you get to the more detailed applications.

Some people in business base their rules of evidence on "gut feel." They believe that intuition is a primary mode of knowledge and validation. Other people want more specific forms of data and statistics as they draw conclusions about what's true and why they think so. They are analytics-driven. Some people look to their own limited experience as primary evidence. For most, it is a combination of many things, and it's a good idea to know what those things are explicitly. Said another way, metaphysics says, "Here is what I believe to be true," while epistemology asks, "How do I know it?" It is powerful to assess how you do indeed know it. If the answer is not satisfying, then it is time to dig deeper.

Let me give you a quick example from one of my businesses. We were selling an "info-product" and were doing so profitably. Our annual sales were in the millions of dollars on this product. We offered a variety of packages at different price points and the margins were solid. We felt pretty smart about it.

One day, I was having a conversation with a longtime dear friend, noted economist Paul Zane Pilzer. Paul is, as they say in Boston, "wicked smaht." He was an economic adviser to two American Presidents and has written many best-selling books, one of which I read years ago and still continue to recommend to this day—*Unlimited Wealth*. Paul also is a very accomplished entrepreneur.

At any rate, Paul and I were talking, and he was explaining to me the concept of "consumer surplus." In essence, consumer surplus is defined as the difference between what a person *did* pay for a particular product or service and what they *would* have paid. For example, if I actually paid $60 for a limo ride to the airport but would have paid $70 for the same ride, the consumer surplus would be $10, meaning the limo company left $10 on the table. I'm sure you probably understand that this surplus can have significant impact on profits since all the costs of delivering, in this case, the car service, is already covered. Let's say there is a $20 profit in delivering the $60 car ride. If you get $10 more, you have just increased your profit 50 percent (from $20 to $30).

Now, this stuff can get quite complicated for simpletons like me. Paul gave me a fifty-page scholarly economics paper on this that he was very excited about. I think I understood a bit more than 50 percent of it, but it got me asking—are we leaving additional profit on the table?

So, I started to do a narrow application of the Philosophy Formula on this.

When it came to this info product's profitability, what did I believe? I believed that we had our pricing dialed in nicely.

Why did I believe that (epistemology)? Well, we sold a "good" volume and we had "good" margins. Looking at these analytics showed it is not an unreasonable conclusion. Maybe the pricing felt good in terms of a gut feel, but how did we arrive at that pricing in the first place?

When we dug into this, I was embarrassed by the answer. We set our pricing solely by looking at what a competitor's pricing was and mimicked it. That is *not* an acceptable answer—the blind leading the blind, perhaps? We likely left massive profits on the table due to this weak answer to the question, "How do we know?"

When I structure my epistemological rules—or rules of evidence—I typically like to apply four criteria (with gut feel maybe a fifth):

1. Deduction: This is the use of logic. From two truths you can derive a third truth. Since it is already in our brains, let's go back to the chiropractic example. Here are the two metaphysical premises/truths:

   The body is self-healing and self-regulating.

   a. The nervous system is the master system and controller of the body.

   Therefore, the logical conclusion is that if you interfere with nervous system function, you interfere with the body's ability to heal and regulate.

   I love the use of deductive logic, but this logic alone is not enough.

2. Induction: Some like to characterize this as another form of logic. This is, for the most part, what people describe as the scientific method—controlled research data on defined groups of people or things that you wish to study. With *deduction*, you are taking general constructs and then applying them to specific situations. With *induction*, you are testing specific situations and applying the results generally. Data from inductive research is a great piece of evidence, but in my mind, many times overrated and incomplete by itself.

3. Outcome Assessment: This is where you are testing and measuring outcomes over time on the specific things you want to know about. This is what my diagnostic technology did. If you had a patient (or customer or client of any variety), you had some logic to the product or service you wanted to provide. You can look to controlled research to say

that this service showed some effectiveness, but then you can find ways to actually measure what's happening to the individuals you are serving. Whether you are providing a product or a service, I believe measuring outcomes to be a critical point of evidence in determining if what you are doing aligns with your what you believe should be happening with your customers. Grabbing a couple of testimonials doesn't cut it. Many businesses have dashboards of analytics, and with some systems, you can measure your outcomes in real time and adapt accordingly. Thinking of the purpose of the business matters here. Many times, we get caught in the trap of revenue and profitability as the things that we primarily want to measure outcomes of, but what about the customer and their satisfaction with what we do? Remember, prosperity is the effect. The philosophy and purpose are the cause. Are you measuring outcomes as they relate to the impact your business is having on your customers or society as a whole?

4. Case Study: I love reading business cases. You can learn a lot by seeing what happens in other businesses. In the clinical world, I am a big fan of the case study. Sometimes detractors would say, "That's weak evidence. It's just a single case. It doesn't matter." To me, those are real patients and real doctors in real battle conditions. It mattered to that patient. That's why I like business cases, too. Deduction is powerful, but a bit abstract. Induction is a bit sterile and rarely mimics the real word. Outcome assessment on your own customers is vital to see how you are doing. Case studies can show you

what is happening with others who do things differently and perhaps more creatively.

In concert, having these four dimensions in your epistemological arsenal is powerful. When I first teach this, for many it is sort of overwhelming, but once the framework is in place and you are asking the three simple Philosophy Formula questions, "What do I believe?", "Why do I believe it?", and coming up next, "What am I going to do about it?", it can get simple and habitual quickly.

What follows is the area that I find cripples entrepreneurs the most—the branch of philosophy known as ethics. Further, when it comes to your brand and the concept of *Your Stand Is Your Brand*, it is in ethics that this all comes together.

Branch 3: Ethics

The subject of ethics runs deep—very deep. The foundation for your brand is developed here. Ethics is the branch of philosophy where your core values are developed and your purpose is derived. These are the nonnegotiable reference points for your brand existence. They are what you take a stand on.

There are the specific aspects of ethics that attend to core values and purpose and there are also the wider aspects that deal with your philosophy of life in general. Of particular interest is ethics as applied to money and value exchange.

This is an area that I have found most human beings, especially entrepreneurs, have some debilitating contradictions in. As we said earlier, ethics provides a human being (or business) with a "code of values" and therefore will be a guide to your actions. This code of values is many times referred to as a "moral code."

I believe most people for the most part, including business owners, want to be ethical. They want to think of themselves as "good," and they want their business to do good things—but what does it mean to be good? What does it mean for a business to do good things? These are questions of ethics. This is why it is essential to identify what your core values are, or in the business context, what the core values of the business are, and let these be a guide to your actions. However, as you'll see in a moment, when you drill down, there are some important considerations that add layers of complexity. To paraphrase Einstein: Make things as simple as possible, but not simpler.

There is a connection between your morality and your spirituality. This is especially true of a business. There is no doubt that there is a "spirit of business." This spirit is brought to light through brand purity. Further, the brand purity arises from the core values, which comes from the foundational branches of philosophy. That's the trail and that is what you and I are building from the ground up through our journey together.

As I said in a previous chapter, purpose emerges from the branch of philosophy known as ethics. This is how philosophy precedes purpose. If the core values of your business guide the choices and actions of that business, which it does (or at least should), these choices and actions will then determine the purpose and direction of your business. (This is also true for your life on the personal side.)

One of the hardest things I had to learn in my own personal philosophy was the moral virtue of capitalism. I found—and find—that the prevailing philosophy toward wealth and value creation in our culture has some glaring contradictions. This results in many successful people harboring an *unearned guilt* that destroys them, either spiritually, materially, or both.

Much of this comes from the moral philosophy of Immanuel Kant and his, what I perceive to be, misguided but effective arguments related to the subject of altruism. In essence, Kant maintains that there is a moral imperative to be of service to our fellow men without reward. In the purest form of this notion, not only would there be no material rewards, but the ultimate moral pinnacle would be to have no spiritual reward, either. Complete selflessness. Pure selflessness is simply not practicable.

When I was in chiropractic school, I would attend seminars and conferences where the leaders would beat it into our heads over and over again that the ultimate moral strata we could reach as healthcare providers was to become selfless servers. There was always this reverence for people in my profession from the past and in the present, who were heralded and celebrated as selfless servers who stood as examples for students to aspire to. Certainly, the ring of it all was quite appealing. Here we were, with our philosophy and our science and our art, ready to go out in the world and help to heal a sick and suffering humanity. We were there not to achieve wealth, riches, or fame. We had a noble purpose, and, in that purpose, we were guided to be completely selfless. So selfless service should certainly be the number one core value of my practice once I started it.

We were taught that in order to be selfless servers we had to remove all financial barriers to our care. We were to accept all patients, regardless of their ability to pay. I remember so often hearing stories of doctors who would give discounted services—even free services—to people experiencing financial hard times. As an aside, the platform speakers who would tell those stories were typically wealthy. I was inspired by those stories, feeling that those people must have been great humanitarians.

I imagine that this particular point of view could be applied to the whole of humanity. Our culture is all about those who sacrifice themselves for the greater good. I left school with this vision, with this motivation, and with the excitement to selflessly serve the sick and suffering. I knew that through my education and skills, I'd be able to do that quite effectively.

I started my practice in a middle- to upper-middle-class town, where most people had some means. They would have an exam and then come back to me in what we called the doctor's report, where I reviewed their findings with them, made recommendations for a care plan, and then went over the pricing. Many times, people told me that they'd needed to think about moving forward and consider whether or not they could afford the services. Following the edicts of what I'd been taught about being a selfless server, I would let the patients know that we had a policy of not letting financial barriers get in the way of treatment.

"What can you afford?" I'd ask them. If I had one hundred different patients, I had one hundred different deals. Although my patient volume was growing and we were seeing a lot of people, it was becoming exhausting. I recall one day, at the end of a fiscal year, I was working on my business goals for the following year. I wrote down that I wanted to double the size of my practice—and instantly had the thought that I would die.

It was beyond exhausting to have countless different deals with countless different patients—not just for me, but for my staff. All of this was occurring under the moral banner that I was a selfless server—and indeed I was, at least partially. The needs of anybody and everybody came before my own, and I was killing myself. All of this—the pain and struggle with my desire to be selfless and making that a core value of the business, my desire to make my moral philosophy of altruism merge with my desire to become financially successful and continue to grow my business—led to a breaking point.

I needed to engage in business training and learn strategies and tactics for being a successful business owner. I joined various coaching and practice management programs in an effort to achieve that. I joined a program called Markson Management Services, and the founder of that program, Dr. Larry Markson, became an important mentor to me. In my early twenties, he exposed me to the mind-set of success. He would tell me repeatedly that "it's all in your head!" In his program, not only did I learn what the headspace was for success, but I also learned the specific processes and procedures that I needed to adopt in my practice to create that success.

As good fate would have it, it was also around this time that I started learning philosophy in the way that I've described in the earlier chapters. I had learned that contradictions lead to destruction. I had an uncommonly successful practice for the short time I'd been in business, but I was simultaneously stressed, burned out, and financially strained. I knew there was a contradiction somewhere and I made it my mission to find it. In that search, one day I found a startling answer. I identified the inherent contradiction and have been digging deeper into understanding it ever since. *I found that my moral contradiction is one that is experienced by the vast majority of people in our culture who are self-made in their success and their wealth.*

An act of altruism is one from which you derive no benefit. You do a selfless act, something from which you receive no gain. Conversely, if you are in business, it *requires* that you make a profit. No profit, no business. Profit, by its very definition, is a gain. So, if you profit, you cannot be selfless, and if you are selfless, you cannot be profiting. You cannot be both selfless and profitable at once. What I found—and continue to find—is that the outcome of this contradiction runs deep and can be extraordinarily devastating. One of two things can happen.

Some people become what I refer to as marginally selfless. They just barely make it month to month, unsure of how they're going to pay their rent or how they're going to feed their families. They make just enough profit to continue to function, but they never get ahead.

Others have created great wealth, but because they have consciously or unconsciously adopted the morality of selflessness, they carry with them an astonishing level of unearned guilt that many times is proportional to the amount of wealth they have accumulated. They are constantly apologetic for the money they've made. If they indulge in nice cars, big homes, or any other displays of success, it's accompanied by guilt, and this guilt many times morphs into an undertone of resentment.

This guilt may exist as a *silent dread*. They are not conscious of it. They haven't thought to themselves, "Oh, I have a contradiction between the morality of altruism and being a capitalist who has earned tremendous wealth. The result of this is that I carry around a guilt, and this guilt is having these adverse effects in all these varying dimensions of my life." However, they do feel angst. They do feel uncomfortable. They never feel settled with their wealth, and they feel like they have to apologize for it. At the same time, they have a desire to spend that wealth, sometimes on business pursuits and sometimes for pure pleasure. That pleasure, however, often comes with guilt, and in many instances, these people are giving away their wealth to charities and other organizations in an effort to alleviate their guilt. They try to convince the rest of the world that they are altruistic at their core. The compulsion being, the bigger my house, the more I need to proclaim to people the amount of money I give to charity. It doesn't work.

The idea of amassing great wealth through value creation, and *not* being apologetic for it, is something they've never considered. As a consequence, they are missing out on both the enjoyment of their wealth and the value they've created in the world. Wealthy capitalists aren't often given a moral sanction, and they deserve one.

Let me be clear here that I believe *voluntarily* contributing to charity is extremely important—when it doesn't hurt you or your business. Under the right set of circumstances, voluntary charity is a very positive aspect of capitalist cultures.

Aligning Material and Spiritual Wealth

Let me share with you how I solved this moral contradiction for myself through years of deliberation, along with where I landed. Keeping aligned with this moral philosophy requires persistent vigilance because so much of the world is not aligned with this understanding and continues to promulgate the constructs of self-sacrifice and altruism.

A sacrifice is when you trade something of greater value for something of lesser value. Some people might say, "Wow, I ended up not getting myself a new car so that I could pay for my kid's college tuition," in the hopes that others would say, "Isn't that great that you made such a sacrifice for your children?" That is *not* a sacrifice in my definition of the term. All this person stated was that they value their child's education more than they value a new car. It would have been a sacrifice if this person had bought himself the new car while valuing his child's education more. That would be a sacrifice—if they had given up their child's education, a greater value, for a new car, a lesser value. So, they can be congratulated for acting on their values, not for sacrifice.

The cult of sacrifice, where people love to put up on a pedestal those who admire the sacrificial altar, has to be eliminated.

Our culture sees that material wealth and spiritual wealth are on two ends of a continuum. This damaged me for years.

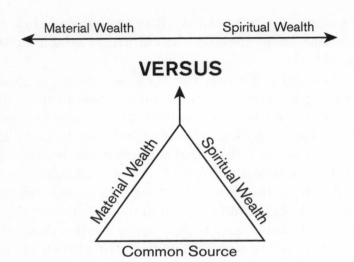

What we are taught is that as you move toward spiritual wealth, you must necessarily move away from material wealth, and as you move toward material wealth, you must move further and further from spiritual wealth. This implies that we have to choose one or the other. Perhaps we could stick ourselves somewhere in the middle and try to be somewhat materially wealthy and somewhat spiritually actualized, but you can't go all out one way or the other. You have to choose.

That's one hell of a choice to have to make. Do you decide that you want to be a spiritually fulfilled and good person, or do you decide that you want to be wealthy and enjoy the finer things in life?

My breakthrough on this was a major one, and it follows the three steps we discussed in the previous chapter. I was struggling with my desire to become more financially successful and reconciling that with my desire to be one of those good doctors—a selfless servant. As I struggled, I had the intention to find a way to resolve this. I read widely in order to peel back the layers of what was known about this subject—what was known about great humanitarians who have made admirable contributions to society; what was known about people who, through their own effort and ingenuity, created great financial successes of themselves.

Amid of this battle between material and spiritual wealth, I happened to be reading Einstein's book on relativity. In it, Einstein stated, "What my equation demonstrates is that matter and energy are both manifestations of the same thing." (Incidentally, how cool would it be to be able to say, "What my equation demonstrates . . . "! I wish I had an equation!)

Consider that for a moment. Energy, or *E*, equals mass, or *M*, times the speed of light squared, *C* (a very big number). My eureka moment struck me so hard and so immediately that it's difficult for me to describe the feeling. Energy represented the spiritual realm. Mass represented the material realm. What Einstein said is that his equation demonstrated, as a breakthrough new view of reality, that matter and energy are both manifestations of the same thing. This immediately extrapolated to me that, philosophically, material wealth and spiritual wealth were not at opposite ends of a continuum—*they were both manifestations of the same thing.* They were not contradictory, they were aligned—different facets of a common source.

When I would explain this to people, whether in lectures or face-to-face, I would get pushback. They'd say things like, "Well, what about Mother Teresa? She took a vow of poverty. She had no material assets, yet she was one of the most spiritual people ever." My response to them is this:

I agree with you that Mother Teresa led a very rich spiritual life. She had an immense impact on sick and suffering people throughout the world. And with her example, she inspired millions more.

But did you ever consider, how does someone who has vowed to be impoverished travel the world to provide such help? What does it take for airplanes, fuel, pilots, food, and other such things to be provided for her spiritual quest? Mother Teresa attracted millions and millions of dollars to her to do her work. This is not a bad thing. This is a great thing. But make no mistake: in the context of resources made available, Mother Teresa was a multimillionaire. If millions of dollars were made available to you in an account that you technically don't own, but do control, so you can do the things in the world that your highest aspirations call you to do, does it matter that you don't personally own the assets?

Write this premise down and repeat it until you understand it. The conclusion that I have drawn solves this moral contradiction. The underpinning of the moral virtue of capitalism is this:

You will attract to you the material resources proportional to the strength of your spiritual purpose. The stronger your spiritual purpose—the thing that you and your business do in this world every day and the reason they exist—the more material resources you will have to actualize that purpose.

There are a lot of "derelicts" who "win the lottery," either through a trust fund or some other method, where they have a great deal of material resources but are absolutely spiritually corrupt. There are also a number of people who decide that their whole life is going to be one of self-indulgence in the sense that they will be dedicated to their own spiritual actualization. They're not adding any value to any other peoples' lives. They're on their own journey in a very insular way. I am not judging it, just stating it.

If you want to see a vision of morality for human beings to exist and coexist in spiritual and material alignment, then look no further than the morality that rewards value creation in a free society. If you are frustrated with the level of prosperity you have, or lack thereof, don't go out and try to figure out "how to make a bunch of money." Get deeper into your purpose and let the material resources flow to you as a result. As I once told a friend of mine who was really in financial trouble when he was trying to decide what to do, my advice was *"double down on purpose."* He did and a couple of years later he was in an unimaginably great financial position.

Referring back to the 5 *Ps*—specifically prosperity. Remember what I showed you? Philosophy and purpose are the cause. That is the spiritual side. Prosperity— material prosperity—is the effect. Material and spiritual wealth manifest from a common source. They do not exist in conflict with each other. Them being opposite poles on a continuum is a fraud. They exist to synergize each other. Doubling down on purpose and expanding is the moral path to greater wealth and prosperity.

I was at a seminar when I heard the following premise, and I adopted it that very minute. It still holds true for me to this day: "The best way to help the poor is to not be one of them."

Do not let the morality of self-sacrifice and altruism destroy any chance you have for material prosperity. Your material prosperity is the means for you to expand the range of a noble purpose in this world. It's the way that you can help the greatest number of people and simultaneously be fulfilled yourself.

At one time or another, many entrepreneurs face a contradiction between the moral and the practical.

Often, we are faced with choices that put us in a seemingly untenable circumstance. We see a "great opportunity," but taking advantage of that opportunity would be in contradiction to one or more of our core values. At this point we feel the conflict. We want to do the right thing and saying yes to this opportunity would be sort of wrong. Then we start to rationalize.

"Well, we would be violating our obligation to our shareholders if we didn't take advantage of this opportunity."

"I need to think of my family, so with regard to my small business, even though this opportunity is not aligned, I need to take advantage of it."

My friend Rick Sapio, whom I mentioned earlier, gave me this edict: *Never take opportunity over values.* Once you start down that road you can end up forever lost.

To recap, answering the following questions can absolutely transform your understanding and action.

When it comes to your personal wealth, what do you believe? Why do you believe it? What are you going to do about it?

When it comes to the product or service your business delivers, what do you believe? Why do you believe it? What are you going to do about it?

When it comes to your love relationship, what do you believe? Why do you believe that? What are you going to do about it?

When it comes to your business success, what do you believe? Why do you believe that? What are you going to do about it?

Here's the point. Often, I pose these questions to people in my live audiences and in workshops. When I ask the question, "What do you believe relative to X?" I typically get an answer that can be accompanied by some stammering. When I ask, "Why do you believe that?", people can get pretty stuck. They get stuck because they recognize that they have adopted premises from their mothers, fathers, teachers, and preachers, and they never independently and clearly developed their own philosophy.

You've been told things during your entire life that you've unwittingly adopted. Now those premises are driving things in your life, either for the good because they are accurate and aligned, or toward a negative place because they are inaccurate and contradictory.

When you were young, maybe you were told that rich people are thieves. If you are unconsciously holding that premise, what do you think you would do about it? Would you want to become rich? Or would you perhaps sabotage yourself?

Maybe you were told that you should not bite off more than you can chew. Maybe you were told that you can't trust other people and that they are always out to screw you over. We all hold views of reality that we picked up along the way. These have morphed into our own philosophies, which in most cases are jumbled and full of contradictions. As a consequence, many of us live in silent dread of doom and inadequacy. That dread remains unconscious and creates a cycle of achievement and destruction that we can never break out of.

Have you ever gotten the feeling that somehow, you're sabotaging the success of your business, the success of your relationships, your parenting, and the achievement of your personal fortunes? I can tell you that I have, and I can tell you that most of the people I encounter through my life share that experience to some degree. The reason is the fog of mixed premises and false generalizations.

By asking these three simple questions—what do I believe, why do I believe it, and what am I going to do about it?—you can break down and transcend these unknown and unseen forces that have been holding you back from who you could be and who you ought to be.

Earlier I mentioned that as a teen I adopted a view of reality that success requires sacrifice. That is what I believed. Had someone asked me why I believed that, my answer would have been because someone I respected told that to me. Yet, that is not a strong enough epistemological position from which to operate your business—or your entire life, for that matter! Someone whom I admired as successful told me sacrifice was necessary. What I did about that was to look for something to sacrifice every time I wanted more success. That was my metaphysical view, my epistemological premise, and my ethical action.

I'm not saying these were conscious thoughts. At that time, I didn't have a conscious philosophy or a framework from which to process these things in my business and career. My metaphysical viewpoint was unconscious. It wasn't until I began learning about philosophy and started to question my premises that I had my breakthrough. Instead of my metaphysical view being that success required sacrifice, I adopted a new view of reality that I could have it all.

When I needed an epistemological reference point to validate that premise, I was able to look for new mentors who *did* have it all and did not believe in the cult of sacrifice being a necessary evil—of having to sell your soul to the devil to have more. The action I took was to work every day to find ways to have it all. It doesn't mean that any of this makes it easy—it just makes it attainable. When I had the wrong philosophical premise, there was no actual path to the life I wanted to lead. The contradiction was between my metaphysical premise and my ethical values. The very nature of sacrifice is the destruction of values.

It's important to understand, especially relative to your personal life *and* your business, that you can focus on these questions in an unlimited way. There are so many dimensions to your life and business—so many varying views that you hold on to. These include everything from the way you hire people and the way you market and promote, to the way you manage the finances of your business, and so on.

Next we need to venture into the important and unavoidable realm of politics. We do this as politics is indeed a branch of philosophy. I am not here to tell you what your politics should be—quite the opposite, in fact. I just want you to consciously understand why you have the political inclinations that you do. There's a great quote from Pericles that would be good to keep in mind as we venture into this realm: "Just because you don't take an interest in politics doesn't mean politics won't take an interest in you."

Branch 4: Politics

Politics is ethics applied to social functions.

You have personally held values. You want to see them adopted by the society you live in. You become an activist and/or choose and vote for a political party that represents these values.

If only it were that easy.

In a business sense, when you identify what your company's core values are and take action on them to effect change on a social level, that's also a form of politics. Many companies take political stands based on their corporate values on things like the environment, gender equality, civil rights, and other such things. It is important to note that your personal values and business values are not the same thing, but they absolutely need to be aligned. Going to work every day to support something you disagree with is a moral contradiction.

Some businesses for good reason may choose not to engage in us-versus-them politics, but I will tell you this—the whole point of this book and its title is about businesses taking a stand based on their values. This doesn't mean take a stand on things for affect. You don't want your stand to be contrived. It means there are real values you and your business care about that you are standing on. (Coincidentally, as I am writing this today with my deadline looming, one of my companies is on the cover of *The Wall Street Journal*, and not in a favorable way, for a stand we are taking. Crazy. I posted about it and basically said, "Just spell my name right, b***h!" I'm taking a stand! The post got a lot of comments and shares. See what I mean?)

Once you know where you are and you know how you know it, and your core values come into play, when you take a stand on those values—a clear stand—and you do it publicly, and your business practices are serving a community of people based on these values, you are having, in a sense, political influence whether you know it or not.

Whole Foods Market and its co-founder and CEO John Mackey have a view of reality, a way of knowing it, and created core values from their ethical views as to what the business would be in the world. It created an entire culture in the society that began to change things. This translated over years to a movement that not only changed consumer behavior but built a $16 billion company that was sold to Amazon. I met John Mackey on a few occasions. He has a brilliant mind and a keen interest in philosophy, and, like me, he is also an admirer of Nathaniel Branden. Philosophy and values drive Mackey. His activism also included his creating the Conscious Capitalism Alliance. I was a proud member of this organization some years back.

I trust that you now have a sense of how ethics turns into politics. Ethics translates into the values your business is holding right now. Politics is when those values start to have social and cultural influence based on the stand you take on them. It doesn't have to relate to the political party of your choosing. It does have to relate to the influence your business has by promulgating clear values into the culture.

I wrestled with whether to mention anything about my own political views here, so rather than people coming to conclusions, let me just say that my political views would fall mostly into the platform called Libertarian, not Republican or Democrat. The polarization today is very troubling. No one is making intellectual or philosophical arguments. It's all quite degenerative in nature and is in some desperate need of healing.

Branch 5: Aesthetics

For many, aesthetics is like a throwaway branch that is more for artists and not businesspeople and entrepreneurs. Here is my view: we are all artists! Every single one of us. In the end, it's all about beauty. Here is a favorite quote of mine from R. Buckminster Fuller:

"When I am working on a problem, I never think about beauty—but when I have finished, if the solution is not beautiful, I know it is wrong."

Beauty is the fundamental nature of the universe. To me, nothing is more beautiful than to see the human spirit shine in the eyes of the visionary entrepreneur who dares to take this energetic thing called an idea and turn it in a material business that creates value in the world every single day, touching and changing lives by the application of values and purpose. Passion, risk, doubt, and the entire hero's journey manifest—what is more beautiful than that?

In the absence of an applied philosophy, when one has contradictory premises, leading to incompatible values that translate into pain and suffering, this all culminates into a conclusion of failure that leaves the one-time passionate entrepreneur feeling that the universe is a capricious, incomprehensible, and unkind place, and further surmising that people either have good luck or bad luck. Most of it is bad. The final result is an embittered future replacing the potential for greatness and joy. Yeah, that's what I understand the impact of an applied philosophy to be. It's the choice between a beautiful future or a resignation of impotence. The nature and purpose of aesthetics is to capture and express these conclusions—this sense of life. Do I see greatness and joy expressed through the art, through the brand, or pain and despair?

Your brand, be it personal or business, is your philosophy manifested through aesthetics. It is every dimension of the experience of your customers, employees, competitors, vendors—everyone who comes in contact with your business. What do they see, read, smell, taste, and touch? Most important, how to they *feel*? Does it purely display the sense of life, the culminated philosophy of the business, or does it confuse them?

Can you see yourself as an artist? Personally, I can't paint or draw at all. I have no talent for sculpting out of clay—but I can conceive and build one hell of a business. It's just a different form of artistic expression. I don't see Jimi Hendrix as a guitarist. I see him as an artist who played guitar. I don't see Steve Jobs as a businessman—he was an artist who built large-scale businesses. Martin Luther King was a passionate artist who built movements.

So, dear reader, please tell me—you are an artist who does what?

To recap, aesthetics is the branch of philosophy where your brand emerges. It is the artistic representation of your philosophical views. What do your values look like? What do your values sound like? If I'm listening to a song on the radio, I don't have to meet the artist to know their sense of life and reality. If I go into a museum and I see a sculpture of a human form and it looks defeated and depraved, or if the figure's chin is skyward and their shoulders are back, I don't have to meet the artist to know what their view of reality and humanity is.

Your visual brand and how you write about your company—how people experience you in every dimension—is an aesthetic representation of your values and your philosophical views as a company. Take Apple, for example. Apple explicitly stated early on that a book *is* judged by its cover. That the quality of what is offered is imputed in the brand aesthetic. In large part, that's what made Apple, Apple.

When that brand is confusing, it means your view of reality is confusing and your values are contradictory. When that brand is clear, whether people agree with it or not, they know your values and what stand you are taking.

This is why *your stand is your brand.*

Now that you understand how to organize your philosophy, let's find your Miles Davis.

Chapter Four

FINDING YOUR MILES DAVIS

How do you know if you have contradictions in your philosophy? How do you know if what is really inside of you—your purpose—is not being expressed? You know it when your feeling about life is, *Where I am is not who I am.*

Laurie and I both enjoy nice meals and good wine. As such, we've eaten at many different and famous restaurants around the world. Never content to always go to the same place, we decided to look for another new spot. I went online to find the newest and hottest restaurants in New York City. I was fortunate enough to come across one called Nomad.

What caught my attention was a video on their website. In it, the manager and the executive chef walked down an alley in New York City and opened a side door to a set of steps that descended into the restaurant. What struck me was that there was no dialogue—just music playing in the background as I watched.

The chef walked through the kitchen, shook someone's hand, and took a taste of soup simmering on a stove. Then the chef and manager exited the kitchen and headed into the dining room. As they did, I saw at a glance a list of core values on the wall next to the door they had just walked through. I froze the frame and took a screenshot so I could read each one of these values.

They were quite unusual, using words like "glamorous," "loose," "enduring," and "satisfaction." As I read them, I began to get a sense of their brand—their vibe, so to speak—based on those words that were their core values. I appreciated that they posted it in a spot that every employee would see as they entered and exited that kitchen—a constant and consistent reminder of their values and of their brand.

I played the rest of the video. The manager and chef continued their walk through the dining room, shaking hands with the patrons. Their interactions, along with the core values, gave me a good sense of what the restaurant might be like. As the video went on, my intrigue for the restaurant grew, and so, though they were quite difficult to get at the time, I booked a reservation.

Unusual as it may seem, I often bring my own wine with me to a restaurant. As I said before, I enjoy world-class wine and have my own collection. Waitstaff have given me a condescending look on more than one occasion, but the reality is that restaurants mark up wines to at least two to three times their retail price and they get it wholesale! They're essentially reselling. Additionally, those wines for which you're overpaying are typically young and aren't ready to drink. It's much more valuable to me to pay the corkage fee for them to open my bottle so I can have exactly what I want, particularly if we're out for a special occasion.

Laurie and I walked into the restaurant and were greeted by a sharp-looking host and hostess. They had the perfect disposition, warm and friendly, without a hint of insincerity. They brought us to our table, and we were greeted by our server, who went by the name Dan.

I waited tables in nice restaurants all through college, so I have a deep appreciation for quality service. It was clear to me that Dan was on the money from the get-go. He took my wine and exclaimed what a beautiful bottle it was, and how he looked forward to opening it for me— far different from the disdain I'd experienced from other waitstaff in other restaurants. He explained the menu in a way that excited us about the food. He was creating an incredible experience right away.

At this point, I wanted to dig in and start interrogating Dan. As soon as I walk into any business where I'm impressed by what I'm experiencing, the first thing I want to do is interrogate the staff to find out what makes them tick. In this case, though, it was my wife's birthday, and I didn't want to take my attention away from her. So, I disciplined myself to refrain from those impulses.

Until she got up to go to the restroom, that is.

That was my chance. I got our server's attention and told him how impressed I was with our experience thus far. I went on to tell him that what brought us to the restaurant was the video I had seen online, and its interesting and unusual core values. "This obviously isn't your first gig as a server," I said to him. "Where did you come from?"

"The owners of this restaurant own Eleven Madison Park," he responded. "I came here to help them open this place."

"I've been to that restaurant," I said. "It's highly revered now because it's a *Michelin* three-star, but I remember when they were a two-star restaurant for years."

Before I go on, let me explain the significance of the *Michelin* star-rating system. *Michelin* is considered by most to be the most credible restaurant rating system in the world. To earn even one *Michelin* star, a restaurant has to be exceptional. In the food world, if a chef is described as a *Michelin*-starred chef, it means they've been an executive chef at a restaurant that has had one or more *Michelin* stars.

If a restaurant earns a two-star rating, they are in very exclusive territory—the restaurant is phenomenal. There are very few in the world. The ultimate rating is three stars. This is legendary. To be a three-star restaurant is to be in rarefied air. According to Open Table, there are over thirty thousand restaurants in New York City, and it would take you 22.7 years to eat at all of them! Of all these, in 2019, only five restaurants in all of New York City attained a *Michelin* three-star rating. There are a little more than one hundred in the entire world. When you become a three-star restaurant, your brand is essentially set up for life.

I continued my conversation with our server, Dan. I told him that I remembered when Eleven Madison Park received its third *Michelin* star. He responded that he was working there when that occurred.

"It was interesting," he said. "Every year, when the *Michelin* star ratings came out, the restaurant strived to get that third star, and they would incrementally upgrade the food presentation and the environment, the table settings, whatever they could. They just kept tweaking here and there to do whatever it took to get over the hurdle keeping them from that third star. One year, the *Michelin* people told the management that if they wanted to become a three-star restaurant, it wasn't going to happen by making incremental or mechanical changes, tweaking little things to get there. They told the owners that they were going to have to *find their Miles Davis.*"

I am not speaking in hyperbole when I tell you that when he said those words, goose bumps covered my entire body, because I understood exactly what they meant. It meant that the owners couldn't fix something outside of themselves to become a three-star restaurant. Instead, they had to dig deeper inside of themselves and find the purest expression of what was inside them. I realized immediately that trying to transcend current limitations, even in a successful business is not a question of what to do—*it's a question of who to be.*

Dan continued, "The owners got together and had a meeting. They decided that they needed to figure out what they could look to that most represented what was in their soul."

What they came up with was The Rolling Stones. Recall their core values—loose, enduring, glamorous, satisfaction. Can you see The Rolling Stones in that? Once they decided to look within themselves to find their Miles Davis and fully expressed it in as pure a form as possible, that is when Eleven Madison Park became a *Michelin* three-star restaurant.

If you, dear reader, want to have a three-star business, or a three-star life, you're going to have to find *your* Miles Davis.

Who to Be—Not What to Do

There are a lot of people out there telling you, "Here's what to do to succeed at this; here's how to succeed at that." The things they're telling you aren't necessarily bad, but I believe those assertions come with inherent limitations.

In the end, you have to dig deeper into who to be, which means you're going to take your stand on the purest expression of what's inside of you. When you are willing, without inhibition, to identify it and let it out, then and only then can you transcend the current status quo and become something much more. Miles Davis stood apart from virtually any other jazz musician for his ability to translate what was inside his soul and put it into music in the purest form possible. It is imperative for you to do the same.

But how?

In order to find your Miles Davis, you must go back to your philosophy. This would include, as we cited in the last chapter, understanding your view of reality. Ask yourself, "What do I believe?" and determine how that is relevant to your business. Understand why you believe it. Emerging from that—and this is the most critical part—are your core values and your statement of purpose. Just as the restaurant Nomad had core values based on a view of life and reality, you need to make sure your core values are reflective of the deepest aspect of your soul or the soul of your business.

Too often, people engage in core values exercises, but the exercises become a trick they play on themselves. I liken it to a corporate exercise where leaders say, "Oh, these words 'integrity' and 'excellence' sound good, let's use those." Those terms are exceedingly common, but they often have no deep-rooted meaning. They simply sound good. I'm not saying that these are bad core values to have, but the question is: Are they really the deepest and purest representation of who you truly are? Are they what matters most?

Once you can get clear on these core values—and clear on this statement of purpose as to why your business exists—and you can state it in a compelling manner that ignites you, then you don't just take those words and throw them in a drawer or hang them on a wall. They become the sheet music that every single person and every single process in your company sings from. Anything—and I do mean *anything*—that does not align with this *must* be changed.

There can be no sacred cows. If you want to play this game all out—if you want a *Michelin* three-star business—everything gets put on the table. You only do things that are in complete alignment with these core values and this purpose, which comes from a deep exploration of your own view of life—your own philosophy.

If you're a business owner, it's critical that you know your core values and purpose as an individual. The core values and purpose of your business don't have to be—and probably shouldn't be—your exact personal values and statement of purpose. They do, however, have to align. As I stated earlier, you cannot go to work every day in a business that is in contradiction to your own personal core values.

Why? Because as I've emphasized a few times in this book, contradictions lead to destruction. No one should come to work in a business where their own personal values are in conflict with the values of the business. As I say, they don't have to match *exactly*, but they can't be in contradiction. When you get clear on this, it's going to become very apparent very quickly which employees in your business need to be promoted and which ones need to go.

Imagine for a moment that every fiber of your personal values are in alignment with the values of the business you have, and every person who shows up to work in your business is also in alignment. You can start to see that you're going to have brand purity—something we'll explore further in the next chapter—that is expressed in every possible way. When you have that, you'll also see that the customers you have are in alignment. That your vendors are in alignment. Everything lines up. That's how you become a "three-star business," if that's what you desire.

One way to look at the relationship between your personal values and the values of the business is this: Consider the business as an entity separate from you. Something that exists in the world, even though you may have birthed it. Much like having a child, you raise it in the context of your personal values, but it has a life of its own, separate from you. It has its own purpose in the world. This is especially critical if you want to have a "sellable" business. It needs to have an identity, a purpose, that is separate, but aligned with yours. I sold my practice over twenty years ago. It is still serving the same community with the same purpose. I sometimes call it the "getting hit by a truck" thought experiment, probably because, as I mentioned in the introduction, I did get hit by a truck. If I get hit by a truck, can this business keep thriving without me? Is its purpose clear enough and strong enough?

Alignment with Shared Values

I highly recommend, depending on the scale of your business, and particularly with smaller businesses, that as a team you create the core values and statement of purpose. This process needs to be led by you as the business owner (if you are the owner), but you will get much better buy-in if everyone participates. To avoid pitfalls of contradictory values that might not align with your own, you can begin with a starter list of thirty values, all of which are somewhat in alignment, and then let the team whittle them down to seven to ten core values. If you're a considerably larger business with perhaps hundreds of employees or more, you'll want to perform this exercise with your executive team, as it would be very difficult to make this process work with hundreds of people.

My experience has been that when you have very clear core values that you are committed to, but you have employees who don't align with them, more often than not, they will self-select out. They're going to feel like they don't belong there. Other employees who *are* aligned with the core values will make those who aren't feel unwelcome, intentionally or not. If right now there are employees popping into your head who you sense are out of alignment, you're probably right. In that case, you need to take action. Do your business and them a favor. Remove them and let them find opportunities in a place that is in better alignment for them. In the long run, it's a win-win for both of you.

As the old saying goes: "It's not the employees you fire that keep you up at night, it's the ones you don't fire that keep you up." Said another way by Rick Sapio, who I mentioned in an earlier chapter, "The definition of eternity is the time between when you know you need to fire an employee and the time you actually do it."

Incidentally, I don't want this to sound heartless. It's quite the opposite. Having an employee in a position that they can't succeed in is as bad for them as it is for the business. As I like to say, "Leaders are people who make hard decisions so everyone benefits." Such is the case here.

Trust the Process

Every so often, I'll run a two-day, one-on-one intensive with business owners that I call Mountain Top Masterminds. Those who participate in this head-to-head consultation come in with the intention of working on core values and related issues. Many times, I will tell them that it takes an outside perspective to help them see their blind spots, which is why people want me to run them through the process.

There are two elements to the process. The first 60 percent consists of working on core values and a statement of purpose. Typically, participants show up with a list of values and a purpose statement, but never once has what they brought come anywhere close to surviving the process. What they bring, for lack of a more elegant term, is a page of bullshit that we have to clean up.

The second part of the process is a *war room* exercise. We engage in getting strategic and tactical in their business. Of course, we can't begin to talk about strategy and tactics until I first know more about their core values and purpose.

This process proves to be transformative for the participants every single time. I've done this for multiple types of businesses, and even though they might be in different industry sectors, the themes and fundamentals are the same. It doesn't matter what kind of business you're in or who you serve. The principles surrounding these concepts are universal.

Here's an example of how simple this can be. I worked with a husband-and-wife team who owned a successful chiropractic practice. They were both very dedicated doctors who had a vision to make a bigger impact. They were already seeing a lot of volume and producing a significant income, but they wanted to contribute more to their community. They came to me and we started the process.

I looked at their core values and their statement of purpose and engaged them in conversation. As I began to dig in a bit, it became clear that what I was seeing on paper and what they were telling me were not aligned. I told them to throw out their original draft, and we started with a clean sheet of paper.

"Let's go find your Miles Davis," I said.

There is a saying attributed to French writer Antoine de Saint-Exupéry: "Perfection isn't when you look at something and say there's nothing left to add. Perfection is when you keep removing things and say there is nothing left to take away."

That is the approach I take when helping clients shape their core values. I take away everything possible, and when there's nothing left to take away, I know we've got it.

When we get to the final list of core values, one thing we have to dig for is the number one core value. The way I describe it to clients is by posing a question to them: If you could only have one value that represents your North Star, one value that sets the tone for all of the other core values and purpose, what would that number one value be? It is critical that it be defined. Once it is, we shape the sequence of the rest of them behind it.

With the husband-and-wife team, what was emerging from their core values, driven largely by the wife, was a very Zen vibe. There was a feeling of tranquility and balance. I saw these words as I was feeling their brand in my head: "ease," "flow," and "balance." I was experiencing it as a thought experiment. It had a spa feel to it—that I was getting out of the stressful world and coming to a place where there is peace and equanimity.

I looked at the couple sitting across from me and said something I meant to be a joke, but it turned out it wasn't one. "So, based on these core values," I said, "when I walk into your office, I'm not hearing rock-and-roll music, right?"

The husband jumped straight up from his chair and said, "I'm not giving up my playlist!"

"What do you mean 'your playlist'?"

He explained that his playlist was mostly '80s rock and roll, and that was the vibe he wanted in the office while he was seeing patients all day. I laughed out loud in spite of myself.

"Why are you going along with all of these core values when it's not what's inside you?" I asked him. "There's nothing wrong with creating the energetic vibe of an '80s rock-and-roll playlist that's playing through the office when your patients come in. However, that's not at all what's represented on the list of core values that we just created. So, what is your Miles Davis?"

If the business has its own independent values, then multiple partners can get aligned with it, and the business has an identity of its own.

It took several more hours to get these two business partners who also happened to be married to reconcile. They had to realize that you can't just go along with core values for the sake of going along and then go to work and contradict it every day. This was an unusually successful chiropractic business to begin with, but the reason they came to me was because they were stuck and wanted to break through. They wanted to go from a two-star to a three-star business.

As is often the case when you are dealing with two or more partners in a business, especially when they are husband and wife, it took a great deal of effort to find the *integrated view of existence* as it pertains to the business. In other words, we needed to find the common philosophy that would allow this entity to be born with a purpose separate from either of them yet aligned with their values.

It wasn't about rock music versus Zen—at least that's not where it started. It was about what they believed was the urgent problem to be facing their community and how the purpose of the business was a solution to that. *That's* the foundation. From there, as we added layers, we arrived at the values that would dictate their brand and customer experience. It was fun and challenging all at the same time. In the end, they were able to build a new foundation, that aligned with *both* of their values, and that is the trick. If the business values are just a cut-and-paste of your own, then the business is you. But if the business has its own independent values, then multiple partners can get aligned with it, and the business has an identity of its own.

This is where alignment is critical. I can tell you confidently for a fact that if you feel like you did this exercise correctly in an hour or two, you're wrong. It takes *deep* soul-searching. Finding your Miles Davis underneath all of the things that have been piled on top of you by your parents, teachers, and preachers is quite difficult. You have to strip all of that away and find the purest form of you and infuse that into the business. When there are multiple partners in the business, then they all need to contribute some of their own "DNA" to create this new thing that represents and aligns with them all.

When that gets expressed, you've reached an entirely new dimension to succeed in your business. Not only on a material level, but to attain the ultimate experience that a business should be, which is an extraordinarily fulfilling *spiritual* experience.

I held a Mastermind session in Nashville, Tennessee, and brought in a guest speaker whom I interviewed in front of the group. His name is Virgil Klunder and he is a wildly successful entrepreneur—so successful that he retired for the first time in his early twenties. Virgil is also one of the most unique and beautiful souls I've ever met. Virgil came to meet me at the hotel where we held the Mastermind session, and while in the elevator, I noted that he was dressed pretty casually, which was fine. Then I looked down.

He was wearing a huge pair of clown shoes. One of Virgil's core values is silliness and fun. If I tried to pull that off, it wouldn't work because that isn't my Miles Davis—but it's his. He's willing to be those things without any reservation about what other people might think, and he's maybe the most successful entrepreneur I know. He expresses himself completely. I'm quite sure he has a genius IQ and he has extraordinary business abilities. He expresses all of that through his Miles Davis, because he doesn't feel the need to hide it. He showed up with those clown shoes because it was the way he wanted to show up, and people were either going to accept it or not, and if not, that was their problem, not his.

The point is that nothing about this can be faked. Miles Davis didn't play what he thought the audience wanted to hear. He played what he himself *needed* to play. The audience came to hear his notes—not theirs.

I created a set of core values and a statement of purpose for this book, and I'd like to share them with you here.

Your Stand Is Your Brand Core Values

- Courage—taking a stand requires courage. It's the ultimate look in the mirror.
- Inspiration—creating the notion of greater possibility for the reader
- Introspection—going deeper "in" to expand further "out"
- Value-Creation—providing immense expansion for the reader
- Impact—new *stands* worldwide can change the world
- Joy—releasing toil and conflict and feeling the bliss of existence as an entrepreneur
- Community—"stand-takers" unite because the whole is greater than the sum of its parts

Statement of Purpose

Your Stand Is Your Brand exists to make manifest the *soul* of business and light a torch for entrepreneurs worldwide so they may experience success, impact, and meaning that otherwise would not be available to them.

Now that you understand finding your Miles Davis, let me give you some examples of businesses that I believe have found theirs, and in doing so, have created what I refer to as "brand purity."

Chapter Five

BRAND PURITY

When a business has found its Miles Davis and starts to express it in all the ways I described in the last chapter, it leads to an outcome I refer to as *brand purity*. In order to understand brand purity, it should be contrasted with brand confusion. These terms are somewhat self-evident, but it will add even further clarity to elaborate on them a bit.

You have brand purity when it's clear what your business stands for, when the values are clear, when the purpose is clear, and everything about the visual brand, marketing copy, customer service, and every aspect of your business reflects the core values and statement of purpose. When you have this brand purity, someone knows quite quickly if they should be a customer of yours or not.

When you have brand confusion, you begin to see that there are contradictions between the values of the company, the operations of the company, the visual brand, the marketing copy, and so forth. In other words, if a potential customer were to land on your website right now, within a short amount of time, they should know whether or not they belong there. Either it's going to draw them in and make them want to explore further, or it's going to repel them and make them say, "This is not for me." That's exactly what you want. If a potential customer lands on your site and *has* to keep digging deeper and deeper to decide if your company is right for them, then you have brand confusion.

Brand confusion is created when you try to be all things to all people—when your values are directed toward trying to cast as wide a net as possible without regard to taking a specific stand. There are plenty of businesses that are profitable with brand confusion, but inevitably, they get stuck, and then they begin to deteriorate. At some point, a company with brand purity that serves a similar sector will take them down.

Businesses that have brand purity create evangelistic customers. They want to spread the word about the business. They want other people like them to come to the business with them.

Consider how people would stand in line for days for Apple products, designer sneakers, or croissant doughnuts. To them it is a duty to the brand to support it in such ways.

If you go back to the very beginning of Apple—which at the time of writing this book is the most valuable company in the world—they started with the famous Markkula document, which was a doctrine of their core values, and it was simple and elegant. Mike Markkula was the first investor in Apple after Steve Jobs and Steve Wozniak. The company desperately needed funding. Markkula brought to the "Steves" a simple one-page document in 1977 titled "The Apple Marketing Philosophy." There were just three values that were the founding core principles, and I contend in large part that made Apple what it is today.

The first core value was *Empathy*, and it was described as truly understanding the needs of the customer better than any other company.

The second core value was *Focus*. In order for them to do a good job on the things they decide to do, they had to eliminate all unimportant opportunities. Steve Jobs once said in an interview that as proud as he was of all the things he did do at Apple, he was most proud of what he didn't do. This speaks volumes about how deeply they held this core value of focus, all the way back to Apple's earliest days.

The third core value was *Impute*, and they described it this way: People *do* judge a book by its cover. We might have the best product, the highest quality, and the most useful software, but if we present them in a slipshod manner, they will be perceived as slipshod. If we present them in a creative, professional manner, we will impute the desired qualities.

The beauty of these core values, on which Apple built the most valuable company in the world, is their power and simplicity. This is a perfect example of eliminating things to a point where there is nothing left to eliminate, which makes it perfect. I give this example because I know that when the idea of brand purity is mentioned, most people immediately think of Apple, and they'd be right to do so. One of the hardest things in the world to accomplish is to hold that kind of brand purity at scale. The bigger a business gets, the more important it is to have discipline around the brand.

Just because this is Apple's way of achieving brand purity does not mean this is right for you. People often make the mistake of trying to mimic other people to create their success. There is a process called "modeling" that the gurus love to assert. It is the idea that if you want to become successful, model other successful people. I'll concede that if you're lost and simply trying to get started, there is some merit to that notion, but you must make sure you are modeling someone or some company's values you admire. However, there comes a point in time where you will have to find your own *Miles Davis*, and modeling someone else's will not work.

I read the Steve Jobs biography by Walter Isaacson, which is a complete masterpiece. A brilliant piece of writing. It was an extraordinarily stimulating look at this enigmatic, amazing person. Having some conversation around this biography with folks in my accountability group, it became clear to me that many people missed the point. Steve Jobs, in his treatment of his employees, his partners, and other important people in his life, was often mean, intimidating, and degrading. The discussion among the accountability participants became, "I'm being too soft on people. I need to be more abrasive. I need to be more like Steve Jobs."

The look on my face was incredulous. "You missed the entire point," I told them. "Steve Jobs was not successful *because* of those particular qualities. He was successful *in spite* of them." Interestingly enough, there was an article in a major business magazine about this very phenomenon. After the biography was released, a number of CEOs turned into real pricks trying to model Steve Jobs, and it was destroying their organizations.

Trying on other people's bad behavior for size is not the way to achieve brand purity or success. That only occurs when you find your Miles Davis and express it *your* way. Let's talk about some examples of companies that have done this.

Why Is There a Penis on Your Label?

Our company Revealed Films worked on a wine documentary in Slovenia, a small country in Europe that was part of the old Yugoslavia. The wine region where we went to do the filming was in an area the Slovenians refer to as Brda (pronounced "birda"), which is right on the border of Italy, near Venice. It was a fascinating area. The lines of the country had been redrawn multiple times in recent history due to wars that affected the region. Many of the vineyards have been part of different countries over time.

The old Yugoslavia was a communist state, and there were constraints on how farmers could produce and what they could do with their wine. That fact was quite formative to the experience of these farmers who were also winemakers. You could say that the political environment did not allow them to express their Miles Davis. After the dissolution of Yugoslavia in 1991, the sons of these winemakers gained a freedom their fathers never had. They now had the opportunity to express their Miles Davis. Coming from a communist environment and then finding such freedom can be a tricky path to navigate.

One of the winemakers I met there had contagious passion and incredible energy—he had absolutely found his Miles Davis. His name was Marko, and his winery was called Dolfo.

Marko is first and foremost a farmer, and we were there during the harvest. As we filmed, I walked through the vineyards with him. We talked about his farming practices. We talked about the "terroir" and what the earth was like and what kinds of characteristics it lends to the fruit and the wine. We talked about the history of the generations before him and what they did there. He had this absolute passion and expression of who he was, what his values were, what his view of reality was, and how it was expressed through the product he created— his wine. He was so passionate about the land and the unique wines he produced, he kept saying to me, "We have nothing to hide."

I had the opportunity, before I ever went to Slovenia, to experience the wines from his vineyard. I was extraordinarily impressed with the wines and their character. They were unique and beautiful, so to say I was excited to actually meet this winemaker and tour his vineyards during the harvest was an understatement. After a full morning of filming in the vineyards, Marko took us all to lunch.

He has quite the interesting logo for his wine right on the label.

Behind me on the wall in this restaurant was a blowup poster of his logo, pictured here:

If you notice, there is a stick figure that looks very loose, almost whimsical, but also there on the stick figure, is a penis. It's worth noting that when he exports to the United States, quite unfortunately, they make him remove the penis from the image because it is somehow deemed pornographic, which makes no sense to me. It's abstract art. Not graphic anatomy.

As Marko described his wines to me, I pointed over my shoulder and said, "Marko, why do you have a penis on this stick figure that's on your label?"

"Because as I'm trying to explain to you," he answered, "we have nothing to hide!"

He would repeat this idea over and over again.

"We want to express the full characteristics of this region," he said, "of this soil, of these wine-making practices exactly as it is without any manipulation to make it anything other than what it is. In the wine-making business, you can do things in the process to try to make your wine more like a French, Italian, or American wine—but we have nothing to hide. That is why I have that logo."

He went on to share, with his thick accent and a passion in his eyes that won't translate to written words, "We are naked. We have nothing to hide. Our wine is pure. The experience in 100 percent clean. What is important is you have to answer the question: What sings for you? So, our wine is dry. Extremely dry. It reflects the soil. The region. And pays tribute to my ancestors."

It reminds me of a Maya Angelou quote: "A bird doesn't sing because it has an answer. It sings because it has a song." Marko is singing his song. That's what finding your Miles Davis is all about and when you express it from your soul all the way to the product your customer enjoys, you now have brand purity.

Marko espoused the purest expression of brand purity, from the soil all the way to the label. Dolfo wines have nothing to hide, and that is their number one core value. When I explained brand purity to him and recited for him how I, as a customer, experienced his brand, he said with watery eyes, "Incredible. You are here and in twenty-four hours you understand my story. How?"

I replied with a smile of gratitude and admiration, while holding a glass of his wine, "Because your story is so clear and so beautiful."

They're No Fools

When we were creating our *Money Revealed* documentary series, we interviewed dozens of experts for the project, exploring this topic at the deepest possible level with some notable people, including Robert Kiyosaki; John Mackey, the co-founder and CEO of Whole Foods; and David Gardner.

My interview with Gardner truly awed me in terms of brand purity. Gardner co-founded the Motley Fool financial services company with his brother, Tom, in 1993. It's likely you've heard of their company as they are in the news and other media quite frequently. You will see the picture of David and Tom with their Motley Fool caps on looking somewhat *foolish*.

I went with my partner and producer, Jeff Hayes, and the film crew to the Motley Fool headquarters in Alexandria, Virginia. It was an impressive and large building that gives the impression of a serious business concern inside. However, once you enter the building and start roaming the halls, you quickly discover that every inch of the facility expresses the core values and brand of the company—there was a lot of "foolishness" to be seen.

The Motley Fool's Core Values:

- Be foolish!
- Do great things together (collaboration)
- Search for the better solution—then top it (innovation)
- Revel in your work (fun)
- Make us proud (honesty)
- Play fair, play hard, play to win (spirit of competition)
- Make foolishness your own (Motley)
- Fill in the blank (write your own core value)

When you land on the Motley Fool website, the first thing you see in the corner is a greeting that reads "Hi, Fool." The overarching theme is one of foolishness, the opposite of what you would expect from a company giving stock advice. Nobody wants to talk about foolishness when they're investing their money, but their approach, their presentation, and their brand purity is nothing short of breathtaking. It's also obviously working because they're an extraordinarily successful company in the crowded marketplace of stock advice.

When I sat down to interview David and the cameras started rolling, the first thing he said to me was, "Thank you for suffering fools gladly. You are surrounded by a lot of foolishness here!"

I asked him about the genesis of this brand. He said that there is no humor or humanness in the arena of Wall Street and stock advice and that he and his brother Tom thought this was wrong. So, he took a theme from act 2, scene 7 of the Shakespeare play, *As You Like It*. This scene references the Motley Fool.

Stay with me—there is a reason for you to understand this.

Tom further related that one of his core values was to tell the truth. Back in the times of the Elizabethan courts, the fools were the only ones who had license to tell the truth in court to the king and queen when nobody else could. How could they avoid the separation of their heads from their shoulders? Through humor.

The Motley Fool's aim is this: Tell the truth. Make people smarter. Use humor.

With all this "foolishness" surrounding me at their headquarters, I couldn't escape the sense of purpose and intelligence that coexisted with it. No one in their "right mind" would venture to start a stock advice and investing business on a platform, culture, and brand immersed in humor and foolishness.

Well, almost no one. David and Tom Gardner did. They found their Miles Davis, didn't let anyone talk them out of it, and achieved a brand purity that has carried them to extraordinary success for decades.

Let me reiterate: if I tried to model what they were doing, if I tried to copy the "foolish" brand, I would fail miserably. It is not my Miles Davis. It's theirs. Motley Fool has received a number of awards for being the best place to work from numerous organizations, including Glassdoor in 2014, the *Washington Business Journal* in 2015, as well as the *Washingtonian* and *The Washington Post*.

What does this all mean? The Motley Fool has very clear core values that have led to a definitive culture in which everyone is engaged. They attract amazingly talented people to work in their company and show up every day aligned with their core values and purpose.

This is a clear expression of what it means when a business finds its Miles Davis. How they play, how they behave—everywhere you look, you see the actualization of their core values and statement of purpose, which has led to an uncommonly successful company that has continued to thrive for more than two decades.

You Can't Fake It

If you think that you'll tactically grow your business by hiding your Miles Davis behind false values—think again. Brand purity *can't* be faked. Any gains that you create when you're not aligned with legitimate core values and a statement of purpose are temporary at best. They're unsustainable. Look at your business and ask yourself, "How can I create more brand purity and take action on that?" Answering that question will have a startling impact on the growth and expansion of your business.

Brand purity *can't* be faked.

That brand purity will take you to your first breakthrough. After that, you'll be hungry for more. We're going to discuss the anatomy of that breakthrough in the next chapter.

Chapter Six

ANATOMY OF A BREAKTHROUGH

My dear friend and entrepreneur extraordinaire Richard Rossi has spent decades in the business of putting on events for high performing high school students—and he has done this very successfully.

Not long ago, he launched a new project called the National Academy of Future Physicians and Medical Scientists. At his inaugural event, he invited Laurie and me to come and get involved in some of the backstage activities. My wife's job was to greet the speakers as they came off the stage and bring them to me. I was tasked with conducting their post-presentation video interview, something for which I have a particularly good skill set.

The event took place in a large venue in Washington, DC, and there were thousands of students in attendance, along with their parents and chaperones. The slate of presenters was staggering. Among them was J. Craig Venter, PhD, who was the recipient of the 2009 National Medal of Science. He and his team were the first to decode the human genome. He is a highly regarded entrepreneur scientist and genomics genius.

Also presenting was the interim surgeon general, Boris Lushniak, MD; Peter Diamandis, MD, the CEO of X Prize; Nobel Laureate Mario Capecchi, PhD; Nobel Laureate Jack Szostak, PhD; Google Science Fair grand-prize winner Brittany Wenger; and the seventeen-year-old phenom Jack Andraka. Jack was the 2012 Intel International Science and Engineering Fair winner. He was fifteen years old when doing this work.

Jack's story is extraordinary, and though it's been seen by the masses on varying television shows and interviews, it is worth repeating here. When Jack was fourteen years old, a family friend to whom he was very close died of pancreatic cancer. The timeline between the diagnosis and his *"uncle's"* death was quite short. As such, Jack decided then and there that he was going to go on a quest to find a way to better detect pancreatic cancer at an earlier stage, with the hopes of sparing others the pain he had experienced in his own life.

It's easy to dismiss this as the wild imaginings of a grief-stricken teenager, but Jack was no normal fifteen-year-old. He was—and is—a person of unusual genius. In speaking to him, it was easy to see the powerful intelligence behind his eyes. It's almost eerie.

Jack began researching and reading everything he could find on pancreatic cancer. Eventually, what he found was that the diagnostic technology used to detect pancreatic cancer had changed very little over the last sixty years. He was astounded by this fact, so he went to work completing a near-exhaustive study of the state of the art in this arena. From the understanding he gained, he began to contemplate innovative methods to find a more sensitive test to detect pancreatic cancer.

As one might imagine, Jack tilted toward the geekier side of the spectrum. His interests were already very much rooted in the scientific world. One day in his high school biology class, Jack was tuned out as he was reading an article under his desk about carbon nanotubes. At the time, this had nothing to do with cancer research—it was just a topic of interest to Jack. In fact, the teacher reprimanded him for not paying attention.

It was at that moment that the proverbial light bulb lit in Jack's mind. He began to imagine how nanotube technology might be utilized for pancreatic cancer detection. With this epiphany, he formulated a hypothesis. The problem was that he needed a lab to test it. Not to be deterred, he wrote up a proposal and sent it out to 200 professors who had labs, complete with a plan, a budget, and a timeline for the project, in the hopes that one of them would grant him the laboratory space to see if his hypothesis held up.

Of those 200 professors, 199 declined his proposal.

One professor—Anirban Maitra—saw something in young Jack's proposal and invited him to his lab for an interview. Jack sufficiently impressed Maitra and his team, and they offered Jack some of their lab space for him to do his work.

In the end, Jack created a method that was 168 times faster than the traditional methods. It was 26,000 times less expensive, 400 times more sensitive, and 90 percent more accurate than what was considered state-of-the-art in pancreatic cancer detection. To say that Jack Andraka had a breakthrough was something of an understatement.

In his *60 Minutes* interview, Jack said that he knew people who were much smarter than him—but he also said this: "You can be a genius, but if you don't have the creativity to put that knowledge to use, then you just have a bunch of knowledge and nothing else. Just like my smartphone."

Why is this relevant here? Because after listening to Andraka's presentation and the presentations of many of the other luminaries at the conference, and after reading books about other giants in history who have created incredible breakthroughs for humanity, I began to see a pattern emerge. As I saw this pattern unfold, I started to look at it from a business and entrepreneurial standpoint. I looked back at my own life and at the case studies of other entrepreneurs, and I realized the pattern was evident there as well.

What I observed was a simple, three-step process that leads to the breakthrough. My intention here, dear reader, is to share this process with you, so you can apply it and have breakthroughs in your own business and life.

Why Do You Need Breakthroughs?

Before I get to the actual process, let's talk about why entrepreneurs, and businesses in general, need breakthroughs.

What's true in biology is also true in business, which is this: You cannot be in growth and defense at the same time. Either you're putting points on the board or you're trying to defend what you've got. There is no sitting still on this continuum between growth and decay. Either your business is growing and moving in a positive direction or it's declining and moving in a negative one. There is no way to squat in one place on the growth/failure continuum, at least not for very long. Some businesses will manage to perch there for a period of time, but like anything else in existence, staying in the same place and holding the line is only temporary. At some point, you're going to end up moving in one direction or the other.

This is why a repeatable process for breakthroughs is critical. When you stop having breakthroughs in your business, you can start to get old and deteriorate pretty quickly. This is nothing new. Many business experts for years have talked about the fact that you have to continue to innovate in order to stay ahead of the competition. You have to generate new and fresh ideas and be creative. You've heard it all before, and the reason you've heard it all before is because it's true. If you're going to grow—if you're going to be creative and innovative and have a future—you must have a process that creates breakthroughs on a continual basis.

I recognized this in my own businesses. In a number of instances, this happens with business leaders and entrepreneurs through innate instinct more than directed purpose. I can say, though, that many times, those instincts dull. Having a template for how breakthroughs occur—to know their anatomy—can be quite useful.

Many of the things that we covered in the preceding chapters will lead to and create breakthroughs for you. You may have had some already. As a matter of fact, if you've been reading up to this point and applying the recommendations and doing the follow-through, you have probably had several significant breakthroughs. If by the outside chance you haven't had a breakthrough, this is the chapter that will get it on track. If you eliminate maximum tension, apply the 5-*P* Expansion Sequence, unleash the power of philosophy, find your Miles Davis, and manifest brand purity, there's no way you won't have considerable breakthroughs in your business. That is my aim for you.

So, let's dive in.

Three Steps to a Breakthrough

Step One: Set an intention.
Step Two: Peel off all the layers of the known.
Step Three: Get some outside inspiration.

With these steps in mind, let's revisit Jack Andraka's story.

Jack started with a clear intention: to devise a much better method for detecting pancreatic cancer so that people who are afflicted have a much higher probability for survival. It's worth mentioning here that when I've looked at many of the cases related to testing my premise around the anatomy of a breakthrough, I've found that a number of the passions that started the process with strong purpose and intention were born out of a serious pain point or compelling need to solve a problem. That is to say, this intention typically has a high degree of spiritual energy behind it, and by spiritual, I mean something that feels purposeful—something important that is attached to deeply held values.

Not everything, however, is world changing. Sometimes you need breakthroughs in mundane areas of your business or life. Let's say you have a certain way of prospecting or marketing. Maybe at present, it's gone flat for you. Maybe the number of leads you're generating has reduced. The way that you've been doing things for years is starting to fade and you need a breakthrough in your marketing. The first thing you have to do is set the intention. What is it, specifically, that you're trying to have a breakthrough around? In this case, perhaps you're looking for a breakthrough in generating volumes of low-cost leads with your marketing. You then study everything that you are doing. Breaking down all the processes, the ad spends, you name it. You are looking for something in the current process that you can improve upon. At best, you have some ideas that, at most, will have minor, incremental impact.

When your mind is in search of a new solution, grinding away, creative ideas that are breakthroughs will be hiding in plain sight.

Then one day, you are at a mall and you see a booth for a local massage clinic where they are giving away a free, five-minute neck massage. You say to yourself, "I've got five minutes." After the sample massage, as you are leaving you see a glass bowl with a sign over it that says, *Drop in your business card to win a free $100 gift certificate.* The bowl is full of cards. Each one of those cards are a lead. If there are twenty cards in there, their lead cost is $5, and since it is a service—meaning there are no hard costs to giving $100 worth of massages—it is even less.

Now you think, *We don't have any contests to generate leads in our process.* You do, however, understand how you can give something away that costs very little, but would be of interest to your prospects, and boom, breakthrough. Contests increase your lead flow by 50 percent and reduce your cost per lead by 70 percent.

If you didn't have the intention, if you didn't peel back the layers of everything you were already doing, you would have walked right by that glass bowl. When your mind is in search of a new solution, grinding away, creative ideas that are breakthroughs will be hiding in plain sight.

Back to Jack.

Jack had his intention and knew what it was he wanted to achieve, so the next step was for him to peel off the layers of the known. What was everything already known about the state of the art in pancreatic cancer detection? What had people been doing and to what degree of success? This meant digging into all the layers of what was known about the current diagnostic procedures. Andraka read everything he could find to understand the known universe of pancreatic cancer detection.

In the same manner as the more mundane marketing example above, your own next step in the process is to peel off all the layers of what you're doing and what you know. What is every part of the process that you're currently using? Who is involved? What activities do they do? You have to know it *all*.

After discovering your intention and determining all that is known about your process, the next step is to get outside inspiration. This is, in some ways, the strangest step, but it's quite consistent, and I am absolutely certain it is critical. The other two alone will not achieve the breakthrough. When someone with a strong intention and a creative, open mind starts to learn everything there is to know about their area of acute interest, there is invariably a separate interest they pursue that causes two worlds to collide to create the breakthrough.

It happened with Andraka. He was reading an article on carbon nanotubes, but not in the pursuit of trying to solve the problem with pancreatic cancer detection. It was a completely separate interest he happened to be exploring. At the same time, he had the reference point of all the known current standards in pancreatic cancer research. With that understanding, as he read about carbon nanotubes, he had his eureka moment. He put those two things together, and a breakthrough was born.

It was like accidentally mixing chocolate and peanut butter, but with even better results.

Brittany Wenger won first place in the Google Science Fair in 2012. In middle school she taught herself to code and matched it to her love of soccer. She created a neural network that taught users how to play.

When she was 15, her cousin was diagnosed with breast cancer. In researching the subject (peeling back the layers), she recognized the need for earlier, more effective cancer detection and set an intention—namely, find an effective way to detect breast cancer earlier. She peeled back the layers of the known.

Then came the "what if" moment of creativity, combining what were two unrelated things for the breakthrough. What if she took her expertise in cloud-based neural networks and applied them to early breast cancer detection? It was her creation of Cloud4Cancer that won her the Google Science Fair Prize. She was able to train the network to have a 99.11 percent accuracy in determining whether a sample of breast tissue is malignant or benign.

Chocolate and peanut butter.

Set an intention. Peel back the layers of the known. Get unrelated outside inspiration.

The thing to understand is this: When you have something that is constantly on your mind—a problem you're trying to solve, or something new in the world that you want to create, it becomes the proverbial burr in your saddle. It won't leave you alone. So you learn everything there is to know about it. You become an expert in that field, whatever it happens to be. Then, you get outside your four walls, out of your traditional routines, and seek outside inspiration. In doing so, you are going to stumble across something that is going to create your eureka moment where that breakthrough occurs. It's almost always something unrelated, outside the sphere of the area of expertise you've developed. Suddenly it all plugs in to give you that "aha!"

This is not accidental. You don't suddenly come to these epiphanies without the other steps occurring first.

One of the most famous breakthroughs to change the course of the world happened with the Manhattan Project. At that time, there was a fear that the Germans were working on a potential weapon of mass destruction that was unprecedented in history, and that if they were able to achieve the creation of this theoretical bomb, they would rule the world with it.

Einstein, who was an avowed pacifist, was convinced by his colleagues to write President Roosevelt and let him know that such a bomb might be possible to create. It was in part due to this letter that the Manhattan Project was born. The project took the most brilliant physicists and engineers in the U.S. and sequestered them with a very clear directive—figure out how to create this weapon, the atomic bomb.

There was a movie starring Paul Newman made about the Manhattan Project called *Fat Man and Little Boy*, the code names for the first two atomic bombs dropped on Japan. One of the big challenges in getting the plutonium bomb to work was achieving detonation. It seemed a hopeless goal. In the film, one day a physicist on the project is eating an orange while contemplating the problem. He squeezes it and sees the juice "explode" out due to the compression. He has a eureka moment and realizes that the way to get detonation to work is by implosion.

I have not verified the accuracy of how the movie portrayed this breakthrough, but it really is a perfect metaphor for what I want you to understand with the concept of the anatomy of a breakthrough. To put it into context, the three phases in this example were:

1. A clear intention to build a working atomic bomb that up till then was just theoretical. The stakes were very high.

2. Peeling off all the layers of the known in atomic physics and engineering. In doing this, they hit one brick wall after another. They couldn't figure out detonation.

3. The outside inspiration of squeezing the orange and making a new connection that didn't exist before, thus creating the breakthrough.

Now I've squeezed a number of oranges in my lifetime and not once did it lead to my creating an unprecedented feat in atomic physics. It wasn't just the squeezing of the orange that was the breakthrough. It was the constant, focused intention of those physicists, then their peeling back of the layers of what was known at the deepest levels in physics. The squeezing of the orange took on new meaning because that scientist's mind was prepared in such a way that the squeeze became an action that led to a breakthrough in understanding.

Breakthroughs Can Be Small or Large

It's important to remember that breakthroughs in your business can be small in nature. They are more times than not. They don't have to be as epic as changing the course of a war, fighting a terminal disease, or winning a world championship. Maybe your breakthrough comes in finding a new and more effective way to hire employees. Maybe it's how you handle conversions in your marketing. Maybe it's an improvement in your cash flow projection. Or maybe it is a major breakthrough where you find a whole new way to offer your product or service to the world.

Breakthroughs can happen at any size or scale. In essence, it is a new or innovative process or understanding that transforms the current status quo. You might be changing the status quo of something that some might not consider all that grand, or you might change the norm of something that is transformative to your entire business or your life.

You'll think what I am about to say is crazy, but now that you're in the process of creating breakthroughs for unprecedented success in your business, let's make plans to burn it all to the ground.

Chapter Seven

CREATIVE DESTRUCTION

At first, you might think this is the craziest thing you've ever read. Here I'm telling you to put in all this effort, energy, thought, sweat, toil, and passion into building something that starts to succeed on an extraordinary level. Then after all of that—after all of the soul-searching and everything else that went into it—I'm suggesting that you burn down some or maybe even all of it and make room for something new.

Yes, it's crazy—but keep reading because I believe in a short while, you'll see why.

A premise I hold and have shared with you in this book is that complacency is death in business. You can't continue to stay the same and expect things not to decline and eventually die. As such, the concept of creative destruction is not destruction in a negative context. It is, in fact, the ultimate act of creativity.

The mythical story of the phoenix is often used as a metaphor. The origin and nature of this widely known myth varies from source to source. After a period of hundreds of years, a mythical bird known as the phoenix perishes in a burst of spontaneous combustion, burning to ashes. Then, out of that pile of ashes, the phoenix emerges anew, vibrant, youthful, and more beautiful than it was before. It repeats this cycle over and over again. Its initial death was seen as tragic, because something beautiful was destroyed, yet out of that destruction arose something more spiritual and powerful.

The story of the phoenix is a relevant metaphor for this notion of creative destruction. When we talk about this concept, it may only refer to a dimension of you or your business—or it might mean the whole damn thing. It doesn't mean you are committing a literal, physical act of terrorism on your business—quite the contrary. What you are engaging in is an act of love and passion. It means that you are willing to let go of how things are for the purpose of creating something greater.

I'll say that again: you must be willing to let go of how things are for the purpose of creating something greater. You must "let go to rise." This was one of the most important lessons I learned, and it happened when I sold the business that I'd started from scratch and ran as its CEO for twenty-three years.

Am I Having a Stroke?

I don't know if you've ever sold a business, but let me tell you, it's a crazy and challenging experience. Most days, you feel like you're running around with your arms waving and your hair on fire (if I had any hair to burn). There are deal points to negotiate. You're dealing with a number of attorneys. You've got impasses along the way during those negotiations. Suddenly the deal is on, then the deal is off, and then it's back on again. You have a couple of ugly conversations with the prospective buyers, then everyone apologizes and gets back on track. Then everyone tells each other to screw off again.

Perhaps some of you have had different experiences with smaller scale, less complicated businesses. However, if you have a business that has some maturity and scale to it, one that you personally built with your own two hands and mind, there are a number of dynamics involved that can make the whole thing a somewhat harrowing experience.

With one particular business, we were getting to a point where the transaction was actually going to happen. Things were on track and the sale was getting ready to close. At the time, I was in Italy. While walking down a street in Tuscany, getting ready to join my wife for lunch, the left side of my body started to get tingly, there was numbness in my left arm. Dizziness set in. At that point, given the symptomatic picture, I thought I was having a stroke.

I was in a foreign country where I didn't speak the language, save some curse words that I learned from my aunts and uncles growing up. Naturally, my anxiety level shot up. Luckily, I happened to be walking with a friend who led me into a store where we called for an ambulance, and I was taken to the hospital. They worked quickly to determine what was happening. My heart was racing. Fortunately, the neurologist there spoke perfect English and assured me they'd run every test to determine what was wrong. In the meantime, they took my history.

I'll be the first to say that my health was and is pretty extraordinary. I took no medications. I was quite fit. I had no history of cardiovascular disease. There was no history of stroke in my family anywhere. Nonetheless, they took my vital signs to find that my blood pressure was up, my pulse was accelerated, and I had numbness, tingling, and disorientation. They ran an MRI of my brain with contrast, along with several other tests. I lay there, waiting for the results, until finally the neurologist entered the room and said, "All your tests have come back negative. I believe that you're having an anxiety attack."

I thought to myself, *Do you know who the f*@$ you're talking to?* I ate stress for breakfast, lunch, *and* dinner. I had never had anxiety in my entire life—cool as a cucumber. To the doctor, I said with considerable surprise, "Me? An anxiety attack?" He smiled almost lovingly and said, "Well, maybe this is the first time for you. Are you under any sort of stress or duress?"

"I'm always under stress and duress," I told him, "but I manage it very well." He then asked me if there was anything happening out of the ordinary. He walked away to leave me to think about his question. I started to contemplate the transaction of the sale of my business, and as I thought about it more deeply, it became an inflection point—a pivotal moment.

Getting to the next level of your life and your career is less about what you need to do and more about what you need to let go of.

I should say that much of this book is about my reflection since the sale of that business. The maturity of the thinking in this book comes from the lessons learned throughout my life, but especially since the sale.

Sitting in that hospital room, I realized that, to a large extent, my entire identity was tied up in being the CEO of that company and the activities of the company. What was happening on a subconscious level is that I was having a complete identity crisis. The actual prospect that this deal was going to close, that the business was going to sell and I'd no longer be involved in it, produced this physical anxiety attack. Once I realized this, it pushed me into deep introspection. The transaction did happen. The business sold, and I had to move on to what I called the third act of my career.

Act One was my chiropractic practice. Act Two was the business, which I was selling. Act Three was going to be things that I had been contemplating for some time, along with working more closely with my wife. We formed a holding company together—Action Potential Holdings—to start a new chapter in our relationship. The old chapter of our relationship had been "divide and conquer." I handled my side of things, she handled her side of things, and together we set out to conquer the world. As mentioned earlier, the new chapter was going to be "combine and conquer."

Letting Go to Rise

My lesson from that health scare is this, dear reader— and I want you to spend some time thinking about it, as I did, because it might be the most valuable takeaway from this entire book: *Getting to the next level of your life and your career is less about what you need to do and more about what you need to let go of.*

I realized that in my own predicament, starting this new chapter of my life, the third act of my career was not about what I needed to do next. It was about what I needed to let go of first. I had to let go not only of the company

I'd built and run for twenty-three years, but on a deeper level, I had to let go of the identity I had—my sense of self—in order to create space and open up possibilities for new things.

In the Philosophy Formula course that I teach, the second module is called Letting Go to Rise. In essence, that concept is what's at play here, at least in part, when it comes to creative destruction. What I'm asking you, right now, is: What do you need to let go of so you can rise?

Like the phoenix.

The process of creative destruction and letting go is not a one-time thing. The scenario I just described about the sale of my business happened almost ten years ago. I had to let go of my identity. Let it burn. I had to go through this creative destruction to reinvent myself and my business activities—my purpose and my vision. Over the year prior to writing this book, I went through it all again.

With my wife's help and coaching, I developed a strong meditation practice. I had quite an interesting experience when I reached a deep level of meditation. I found myself in a zone of being in a place where there was really almost no time and space. Barely on the edge of awareness, I found that I became an almost third-party viewer of myself. I witnessed burning within me, from the bottom of my neck down to my pelvis, in my entire chest cavity. Energetically speaking, there was a bonfire burning.

I know, you came to this book for business advice, but bear with me. At first, when I witnessed this, I wasn't sure what to make of it. I wasn't afraid of it, but at the same time, I didn't understand what was burning. Over time, I realized that it was my sense of identity burning and it was a raging fire. Rather than try to resist it, and rather than try to put the fire out, I listened to a little voice that kept whispering to me, "Let it burn. Just sit back and let it burn."

Over time, I took comfort in the flames, realizing that this was a necessary process—something that I had to surrender to and let happen throughout the period of almost a year, until it finally did burn down. That was the edict, the sense of the voice that whispered to me to let it completely burn to ash. Out of the ash, a new thing would rise—this phoenix, the next chapter of my expression.

Commensurate with that was the acceptance of my proposal for this book and my becoming a first-time author, finally writing a book after all these years. I don't yet know how much this process is in alignment with the magical mystery of life or how things will unfold. I was a force-of-will entrepreneur, a self-made man who takes the world and shapes it into the way he sees it, a man who was willing to run through brick walls and fight all of the battles necessary to succeed in the world. It was something I'd spent decades doing. I did so only to find out how beat up and broken one can end up as a consequence. There is no doubt that the force of your own will can make things happen—but there is also no doubt that it alone is inherently limited. Just like any drug that can *force* your blood pressure to lower or *make* your cholesterol go down, those same drugs will have adverse side effects and consequences that are not desirable.

I believe that all of this is an evolutionary process of the human spirit and experience. Learning and understanding how to surrender and let go comes from a unique form of strength and can sometimes—I dare say most times—be much more powerful and expansive than the force of will, particularly when it comes to outcomes. When I talk about creative destruction, I'm talking about this idea of a willingness to let a current sense of identity and way of doing things burn down so that something bigger and more powerful can emerge.

Back to Eleven

Recall how I discovered what it meant to find your Miles Davis back at Eleven Madison Park—the one-time two-star *Michelin* restaurant striving for its third star. The story didn't end once they achieved it.

Over a period of years, not only were they in the rarefied air of being a *Michelin* three-star restaurant, but they took it a step further. Recently, as referenced to the time of the writing of this book, Eleven Madison Park was voted the number one restaurant in the world. Not only did they have their three-stars, but they were considered the best of even those other three star establishments. As you can imagine, when you're recognized as the number one restaurant in the world, you're going to have a waiting list almost every night of the week. You can raise your prices and ride that out for years and years—and rightfully so. You've earned it due to your achievement.

Shortly after they achieved this extraordinary acknowledgment and award, do you know what they did?

They closed the restaurant down in order to "burn it down" to start from scratch and recreate the whole thing. Again, to most, this would be the craziest thing a business could ever do. They had achieved so much and could monetize it for almost as long as they wanted, yet they decided to burn it all down and reinvent themselves. Same restaurant, same name, but when the chef co-owner Daniel Humm and his business partner, Will Guidara, were interviewed about why they were doing this, they answered that their philosophy was that you can never stay the same and stay on top. You have to constantly reinvent yourself.

To quote Humm: "In a way, it was kind of a beautiful thing. Kind of unexpected. Maybe it's not the smartest thing from a business point of view, you know, closing when you have the most demand, but in a way it's kind of badass, too."

You have to be creatively destructive.

It's a fascinating story in so many ways. They took all the metal, the pots, and the pans from the kitchen and had it all melted down and reformed into a step that's at the front of the restaurant. Humm stated that every time people come into their establishment, they're stepping over the past and into the future.

The type of person or people that it takes to start a restaurant, build it over years, and have it become the number one restaurant in the world are the same type of badasses who, once they achieved it, decide to burn it all down and create something new. They would do this in spite of many people telling them how foolish they were—how they should have kept a good thing going and should have kept on cashing those checks. The type of person who would have thought that way would never have taken the restaurant to number one in the first place. Only someone prepared to tear it all down has the mentality to take something to those great heights.

They let go to rise again—for the possibility of an even better, more beautiful Eleven Madison Park. Was it a great risk? Yes. Is it possible that the critics won't like the new restaurant as much, and could it lose much of its social esteem? Quite possibly. However, I can tell you that when I saw the interview with the executive chef co-owner Daniel Humm, I was looking at one of the freest human beings I'd ever seen in my life. He was unattached.

It's our attachments that confine us. It's our attachments that limit us. It's our attachments that put boundaries around our freedom. In that interview I saw a human being who was as free as any human being I'd ever known. He had achieved great things, yet he was untethered by the social self-esteem that went with those achievements. He was someone who knew how to surrender, let go, and to rise.

Lonely Hearts

I'm sure you've heard the term "Beatlemania."

If you know the story of The Beatles, you know that they were big in Europe, and when they came to the United States and appeared on *The Ed Sullivan Show*, the phenomenon called Beatlemania ensued. If you look back at any of the old stadium concerts they performed at the height of that craze, which are things of legend, the arenas were sold out. The crowds screamed so loudly, you could barely hear the music at all. Mania was an understatement.

Beatlemania had such a fervor attached to it that it was practically immeasurable. These four working-class kids who'd grown up in Liverpool, England, suddenly became the biggest musical phenomenon the world had ever seen. They were thrown into unprecedented superstardom and the accompanying wealth that went with it.

John, Paul, George, and Ringo were cultural icons with an identifiable brand signature that encompassed their look and their sound. They were the biggest musical brand in the world—The Beatles—the four "mop tops" with their Beatles haircuts and Beatles suits. At their peak of fame with many more venues to be sold out, and much more money to be made, what did they do?

They quit touring—stopped it altogether. They disappeared into the studio, and after a great deal of time had passed (they spent more than thirty times the amount of time on this album as compared to the first one they did), they reemerged with something that had never been done before: they had recorded a concept album. That album was *Sgt. Pepper's Lonely Hearts Club Band.*

Not only did they not sound the same, they also didn't look the same when they returned to the scene. Now The Beatles had long hair, beards, and mustaches, a far cry from the mod haircuts and black suits that everyone associated with Beatlemania. They burned their old identity to the ground at the pinnacle of their success. What they surfaced with was something completely new, creative, and different. In fact, many audiophiles to this day consider *Sgt. Pepper* to be the greatest album of all time. *The New York Times* music critic panned the album when it debuted. He hated it. In an interview on the fiftieth anniversary of the album, he said something to the effect of, "Yeah, I got that one wrong." He said it was just so different and such a departure with all of these long songs that kind of ran into each other that he just didn't get it at the time. He gets it now. It changed the face of music.

If The Beatles had decided to run out their success, clinging to the identity that accompanied Beatlemania, there never would have been a *Sgt. Pepper* and all of the incredible work that came after it by them and many other bands that the album absolutely influenced. Most consider The Beatles to be the greatest rock band of all time, and you can include me in that category. The reason they hold this title and why no one will ever replace them is because not only were they responsible for the greatest music phenomenon of all time, but they were willing to burn it all down and reinvent themselves, over and over again.

This is the nature of creative destruction. It's not for everyone and it's certainly not for the faint of heart. Maybe you've got a good thing going at the moment. Maybe you even have a mediocre thing going that sort of pays the bills. What I can tell you is that if you want to have a true journey in your life and in your career—if you want to explore the depths of what's possible for you and your business and you want to have multifaceted, multilayered life experience, then creative destruction is the only way to make that happen.

I've seen lecturers, authors, and thought leaders who give the same signature lecture with the same concepts for decades on end. They struck gold forty years ago with a certain conceit, a certain theme or idea, and their entire life and career continued on the same circuit, talking about the same thing. I'm not saying there's anything wrong with it. I'm not saying they weren't able to be financially successful and help people through their work. What I do know is that it isn't the journey for me.

The biggest compliment I get when I'm out lecturing these days is from people who have followed me for decades. They will walk up to me and say, "My goodness, you've reinvented yourself again." As of the time of this writing, I gave a talk in a large auditorium with approximately three thousand people in attendance. Many had seen me speak time and again at an event called Cal Jam, which I feel quite connected to.

Cal Jam is a fascinating event, founded by Dr. Billy DeMoss and his companion, Mary Jane, who have become close friends. He was another perfect example of finding your Miles Davis. He had two loves in his life, one of which was rock-and-roll music, and the other the chiropractic profession and natural healthcare. So, he organized an event with a live band on stage playing fantastic rock and roll between each speaker. The spark and energy of this event is such that it feels like a revolution. You have people there committed to a vision and a cause—they want to make the world a healthier place.

Many great speakers attend this platform. A distinction I have is that I'm the only speaker who has presented at every single Cal Jam event for more than a decade. I have never given the same talk twice. Based on the bonfire that raged inside me, my old identity burning down, and a new one emerging, when I stepped to the stage this past time, my talk was even more different still. The message was nothing like anything I'd ever presented before. The energy had shifted in a very different way.

This can be a bit unnerving because you're known for a certain thing. People have their expectations when they come to hear you speak. I imagine, on a much grander scale, when The Beatles released *Sgt. Pepper* that they were proud of the album and loved it, but they might have had some concerns about how the world was going to receive it after Beatlemania.

I held that same concern regarding people's expectations, but I didn't let it derail my intention for the talk. I didn't rally them as strongly as I normally would have. They didn't get as fired up as they did in some of my other presentations. I had to push all that aside and recognize that this was a different talk for a different purpose coming from a different person—one who had shifted his identity to something new, which was less high-pitched motivation and more deep contemplation and inward reflection.

You have to let go to rise. Creative destruction is the path where you can burn down the old identity and old way of doing things and let something more powerful, more beautiful, and more evolved emerge from those ashes.

As we near the end of this particular journey together, I feel it would be critical to be a bit vulnerable and share some of the more intimate aspects of my personal life. By now I think you see that the principles I share in this book aren't just for business; they apply to your entire life. Even the most precious and intimate areas of it. Knowing your values, having a vision, and taking a stand in my marriage has been transformative. Relationships were a very rocky road for me based on bad premises, which led to regrettable decisions and toxic outcomes. What good is great business achievement if the other areas of your life fail? Too many entrepreneurs suffer in the most humanistic areas of their lives where real joy and fulfillment should exist. So let me share with you as a final thought how, with my wife, I learned to combine and conquer.

CONCLUSION

Combine and Conquer

It's time for us to bring our experience together full circle—and also time for us to connect on a deeper level and get more personal.

In the introduction of this book, I shared with you a stand that I took that was quite polarizing. Doing so led to a magic carpet ride that, in part, resulted in this book being written. Now I'd like to share with you in a more in-depth regard how we—my wife, soul mate, and business partner, Laurie, and I—took the concept of taking a stand into our personal lives. If I can do a compelling job of that here with you, it is my hope that together we can create a community of "stand-takers." Not only do we want to know what our stand is as individuals, we want to express the stand we take as a community.

Our story involves hospital visits, letting go of old identities, reinventing a way to experience life, the formation of new businesses, and some pretty badass tattoos. Let us explain.

Recall when I was walking down the street in Tuscany, thinking I was in the midst of a stroke, only to find out I was having my first panic attack. While lying on my back in that hospital, wondering how the hell I let myself get to this point, I also had tears of gratitude

YOUR STAND IS YOUR BRAND

streaming down my face for the life that I had. There is nothing like an emergency hospital visit to snap you into some deep introspection.

I realized that by selling the company I co-founded and ran as CEO for more than two decades, I was also selling my identity. As I started to weigh that against the gratitude I had in my life for my family, I also recognized an opportunity was presented for me to have a new, better, and more transformative experience with my wife. In order for that to happen, however, Patrick the entrepreneur and business leader who went out on a daily basis to slay dragons had to die. A new Patrick had to show up—one that wanted to be less of a dictator and more of a collaborator.

> **Taking a stand is about knowing your values clearly and expressing them fully, independent of how others might judge you.**

As I mentioned earlier, Laurie and I put our heads together and formed a new entity—a holding company we named Action Potential Holdings.

No Sacrifices, No Pain

Along the path to the concept and formation of that entity, Laurie had a number of critical distinctions that we would like to share here. This is the way we decided that based on our values, and the vision we had for our relationship, that our new venture together was the best for us. This type of husband-and-wife collaboration may or may not be the right thing for you, but understanding the distinctions that we made along the way to land where we did—whether it is exactly the same way you want to do it or not—can make a significant difference in your life.

When you think about it in the end, what good is taking your stand or building an incredibly successful business if it creates alienation and breakdown in the deeper and more important areas of your life? If you've learned nothing else from reading this book, I hope you've learned that taking a stand isn't about creating sacrifices and pain in your life. Taking a stand is about knowing your values clearly and expressing them fully, independent of how others might judge you.

So often, we have preconceived notions around what it takes to have a successful life. As I've stated in earlier chapters, many of these notions are unconscious to us. They come from parents, teachers, and preachers, and we live them at great peril because they are unexamined. If you've read this far, I'm sure you now understand the power, importance, and significance of living consciously, and identifying the values that lead you to a purpose and taking your stand.

You Can Have It All

You might ask, "But what if doing so disconnects me from my spouse? What if it disconnects me from my kids and my other important relationships?"

Recall that at some point I reached a significant turning point in my life and career when I realized that I could have it all. You can, too, but having it all means getting together with your spouse and shaping these things collaboratively. In my previous business life, I always drove these things individually. As a matter of fact, I was in successful and growing businesses when I met Laurie, so obviously up till then, I had to create that without her.

After twenty-three years in business, I could have decided to go another twenty-three years on the same track. I shudder to think what my life would be like today had that been my decision. Why? Because I realized that not only did I want to take a new stand in my career, but through Laurie's wisdom, encouragement, and vision, I realized there was a new stand to take in my marriage.

We, Together

I mentioned some of this earlier in the book, but now let's explore it in its wider context. Laurie said it best when she said that up until that point, we'd lived by a driving premise of "Divide and Conquer." In that mentality, you've got little babies and you've got growing and demanding entrepreneurial businesses. You've also got all of the other accompanying things that cause one marriage partner to have to handle the home front so the other marriage partner can go out and be the provider and make the living. Then at times, you take your vacations and you amalgamate your family, but that is the exception, not the rule.

The rule is division. The rule is divide. In hindsight I can now say that what my wife saw the whole time was that division was antithetical to the vision of a marriage we wanted to have. You don't divide and conquer and have a legendary romance.

Some people might have different values in their relationships. Maybe the whole idea of their relationship is to divide and conquer because there are certain bases they want covered—the quantitative and qualitative time they spend together is not that important. It's only about creating successful outcomes. It's just about raising the kids and getting them into decent colleges. It's just about having some degree of wealth and security. If between the two marriage partners all the bases can get covered, that might be what they consider successful. There's no "one size fits all," and this looks different for everyone.

When the opportunity presented itself to sell the business, Laurie said that she wanted us to go from the premise of "divide and conquer" to the new foundational premise of "combine and conquer." She wanted us to go from facing each other to now turning shoulder to shoulder, facing the *world* together. In order to do this in a meaningful way, it would mean taking the opportunity to sell my company—taking a figurative clean sheet of paper and together determining the core values of what would be our new company.

We, together, would determine the vision we had for it. We, together, share in the purpose that fuels it all. We spent a good amount of time shaping all of this—Laurie acting as a magical muse, constantly stimulating the vision of possibilities, and making it fun and exciting; and me being the philosopher entrepreneur, organizing it and putting it on the ground.

After going through all the fun of hiring graphic artists, creating a visual brand around our values, and coming up with our succinct definition of purpose, we sat with it for a while. When we felt like it was locked and loaded, we did the unthinkable at our relatively advanced ages—we took our brand logo and decided to get it tattooed on the back of our right shoulders, permanently sealing our intentions. Laurie said it was a fitting metaphor that as we stand shoulder to shoulder, facing the world, anyone in front of us would see us standing together. Anyone behind us would see tattooed on us the symbol of our purpose as we stand and face our future together.

Of course, dealing with our children, getting them to understand why Mommy and Daddy are suddenly going out and getting tattoos, was a more than interesting exercise in and of itself—but that's a story for another book.

We're not sure what's right for your life, or what's right for your premises around how you bring together your career and your personal life. However, we invite you to consider the possibility of what it might mean for you and your business if you face the world together rather than being divided to conquer it.

Enliven Humanity

It took us a while to arrive at the stand that we decided to take, but when we thought about our values and what we wanted all our activities to point to, it added up to a two-word statement of purpose: *enliven humanity.*

We had deep, meaningful conversations around what was going on in the world, what kind of challenges it faces, and what kind of role we wanted to play. We couldn't escape the conclusion that most of the world is sleep-walking. People are tied to a sense of life that they never consciously adopted. They live by premises that they don't know or understand. They never consciously chose their values and they don't take a stand, which is a uniquely human thing to do.

Instead, they're on the treadmill, grinding it out, day by day, grabbing any chance pleasure that came along the way and hoping to avoid whatever pain might come their way. That, to us, was not living a truly human existence. We wanted to wake people up. We wanted to enliven humanity.

If you'd like to check out the core values we created for Action Potential Holdings, I invite you to go to this book's companion site, YourStandIsYourBrand.com. There are a number of materials, pictures, free downloads, and other such things waiting there for you.

What's *Your* Stand?

Now that we've shared our stand and purpose with you, we invite you do the same.

There is an old proverb that says that when you save one life, you save the entire world. We share this with you because we want you to understand that your stand doesn't need to be something grandiose and epic in scale. As a matter of fact, I suggest for most people that maybe it shouldn't be. Your stand can be something very simple, but very meaningful to you. I further contend that by sharing your stand, however small, it could be quite meaningful to someone else. To paraphrase that proverb, if you've changed one life with it, then you've changed the entire world.

I want to present you with an opportunity—a win-win one at that. I invite you to visit YourStandIsYour-Brand.com, and once you get there, I invite you to join the community of stand-takers, and I want you to share your stand. I want you to witness the stand that others are taking and to stay engaged with this work so that together we can enliven humanity. When you reach the site, enter the code "istand" to receive a free gift—a little something extra from us to you.

If this book has meant something to you, then let this not be the conclusion of our experience together, but the beginning. It's been a privilege to stand with you during this journey.

ACKNOWLEDGMENTS

As I begin to consider that proper scope of the acknowledgments I'd like to give, I realize that it would require another book! Over time I have come to recognize the complex and beautiful web of connections that leads us to this present moment. One thing leads to another, to another, to another, and in sum total, for better or for worse, here we are. So in acknowledgment, I have to start with my extraordinary wife, Laurie, who came up with the title, *Your Stand Is Your Brand*. We were sitting at a café over coffee in LA as I was contemplating a lecture I was to give at a large convention, explaining the moral and practical virtue of businesses taking a stand and how that creates their brand identity and culture. I was droning on and then she just simply looked at me and said, "So, your stand is your brand." How she can always see simply and clearly what I tend to complicate. The lecture was a big hit. She's my muse.

Growing up as a kid in New Jersey, the youngest of three, I was blessed. My father, Patrick, a World War II vet, has passed, but his support of my crazy ideas, even when he disagreed with them, was crucial. My mother, Antoinette, literally shaped my thinking. She taught me to believe in myself. That I could achieve anything I put my mind and will to. She said, "When you talk to yourself, watch your language!" I was a two-time AAU national karate champion. At the first nationals, after I won the first of my seven fights, I asked her, "How do you think I'll do today?" She responded, "You've already won, it's just a matter of time before it happens." She taught me to win in my mind first. I apply that to this day decades later. My brother Joseph and sister Vicki are the best siblings imaginable. Loving. Supportive. Cheering for me. Without them I'd be lost.

This book wouldn't have happened without my longtime, dear friend Dr. Joe Mercola. He brought me as a guest to a Hay House authors' mastermind where I gave a brief presentation mentioning the concept of Your Stand Is Your Brand. It really got the attention of the room. So thank you, Joe! And thank you, Patty Gift and Reid Tracy, for witnessing the concept live and believing in the prospects of this book! I also want to acknowledge the entire Hay House team who work with passion and competence.

I have had too many intellectual and success mentors to mention them all. Dr. Nathaniel Branden, even though he has passed, his wisdom lives in me each day. Dr. Christopher Kent, one gets smarter just being in the same room as you. Dr. Larry Markson, your teachings on success have stood the test of time, as has your impact. Paul Zane Pilzer, your books and friendship have always been like sunshine and water on a well-rooted plant. Jeff Hays, your wisdom and friendship knows no bounds and continues to deeply touch me and countless others.

John McVie, thank you not only for your loving friendship and generosity, but also for the tickets to all those gigs! Through example, you've inspired me and taught me that one can stay humble and thoughtful even after decades of world-class excellence and success on the highest levels. You are a rock-star human being.

Acknowledgments

My children, Connor, Antoinette, and Hudson, you inspire me, humble me, and bring incalculable joy, love, and meaning to my life.

This book never would have happened without the work of the world's best "Scribe," John Vercher. Thank you!

To all the mentors, best friends, accountability partners, and inspirations in my life. You know who you are. Let me simply say you are loved and very appreciated.

ABOUT THE AUTHOR

Patrick Gentempo is a serial entrepreneur who has founded and led multiple multi-million-dollar companies. Early in his career as a practicing chiropractor, he co-developed diagnostic technologies, for which he received multiple patents. With his decades of experience having founded and co-founded over 15 businesses in various fields ranging from diagnostics to filmmaking, Dr. Gentempo has mastered a specialized skill in the practical application of philosophy in business. A celebrated international speaker, he has been published by Forbes.com, has testified in front of Congress on the use of technology in healthcare, given testimony to the White House Commission on Complementary and Alternative Medicine, and received numerous business and healthcare awards. He lives in Park City, Utah, with his wife, Laurie, and his three children, Connor, Antoinette, and Hudson. You can visit him online at www.Gentempo.com.

We hope you enjoyed this Hay House book. If you'd like to receive our online catalog featuring additional information on Hay House books and products, or if you'd like to find out more about the Hay Foundation, please contact:

Hay House, Inc., P.O. Box 5100, Carlsbad, CA 92018-5100
(760) 431-7695 or (800) 654-5126
(760) 431-6948 (fax) or (800) 650-5115 (fax)
www.hayhouse.com® • www.hayfoundation.org

———

Published in Australia by: Hay House Australia Pty. Ltd.,
18/36 Ralph St., Alexandria NSW 2015
Phone: 612-9669-4299 • *Fax:* 612-9669-4144
www.hayhouse.com.au

Published in the United Kingdom by: Hay House UK, Ltd.,
The Sixth Floor, Watson House, 54 Baker Street, London W1U 7BU
Phone: +44 (0)20 3927 7290 • *Fax:* +44 (0)20 3927 7291
www.hayhouse.co.uk

Published in India by: Hay House Publishers India,
Muskaan Complex, Plot No. 3, B-2, Vasant Kunj, New Delhi 110 070
Phone: 91-11-4176-1620 • *Fax:* 91-11-4176-1630
www.hayhouse.co.in

———

Access New Knowledge.
Anytime. Anywhere.

Learn and evolve at your own pace
with the world's leading experts.

www.hayhouseU.com

Listen. Learn. Transform.

Listen to the audio version of this book for FREE!

Today, life is more hectic than ever—so you deserve on-demand and on-the-go solutions that inspire growth, center your mind, and support your well-being.

Introducing the *Hay House Unlimited Audio* mobile app. Now you can listen to this book (and countless others)—without having to restructure your day.

With your membership, you can:

- Enjoy over 30,000 hours of audio from your favorite authors.
- Explore audiobooks, meditations, Hay House Radio episodes, podcasts, and more.
- Listen anytime and anywhere with offline listening.
- Access exclusive audios you won't find anywhere else.

Try FREE for 7 days!

Visit **hayhouse.com/unlimited** to start your free trial and get one step closer to living your best life.

FREE WEEKLY BUSINESS INSIGHTS
from a MASTER IN THE FIELD

 Over the past 30+ years, Reid Tracy, President and CEO of Hay House, Inc., has developed an independent upstart company with a single book into the world leader of transformational publishing with thousands of titles in print and products ranging from books to audio programs to online courses and more.

◆ Reid has dedicated himself to **helping authors create successful businesses around their books and vice versa,** and now he's here to help you achieve success by guiding you to examine and grow the business best suited to you.

◆ The Hay House Business newsletter isn't just about book publishing or becoming an author. It is about **creating and succeeding with your business and brand.**

◆ Whether you are already established or are just getting your business off the ground, the **practical tips delivered to your inbox every week** are invaluable and insightful.

Sign up for the Hay House Business newsletter, and you'll be the first to know which authors are sharing their wisdom and market-tested experience with self-starters and small business owners like yourself!

Sign Up Now!
Visit www.hayhouse.com/newsletters/business to sign up for the Hay House Business newsletter.